CERERBRATE!

Oracle Guidance From Your Angels

By Chaplain Jodi Dehn

Published by Tamerlane Media, LLC

Copyright 2024

While every precaution has been taken in the preparation of this book, the publisher assumes no responsibility for errors or omissions, or for damages resulting from the use of the information contained herein.

CEREBRATE! ORACLE GUIDANCE FROM YOUR ANGELS

First edition. May 13, 2024.

Copyright © 2024 CH Jodi M Dehn.

ISBN: 979-8989852413

Written by CH Jodi M Dehn.

Table of Contents

SECTION ONE

Time to Cerebrate! How to Use This Book

Cerebrations are moments of profound thought, those instances where the mind engages in contemplation, reflection, and realization. In this book, we embark on a journey through the realms of thought, exploring the transformative power of angels—non-religious, genderless energies that exist to support and guide you through life's challenges.

Life is a tapestry woven with both joyous moments and challenging struggles. It is during these life struggles and traumas that we often seek solace and guidance. Within the pages of this book, you will discover a unique approach to finding support and strength – the utilization of angels as powerful allies on your life's journey.

These angels are not bound by religious affiliations; instead, they are ethereal energies radiating light and love. Their purpose is to communicate messages that inspire, heal, and uplift. This book serves as a guide to help you connect with these benevolent beings, tapping into their wisdom to improve your day-to-day life.

The essence of this guide lies in the understanding that angels are ever-present, patiently waiting for you to open yourself to their messages. Through their guidance, you can navigate challenges with newfound resilience and perspective.

How to Use This Book:

1. Openness to Receive: Begin by cultivating an open mind and heart. The angels are always with you, but their messages become clearer when you are receptive to their guidance. Approach this book with an eagerness to explore and an openness to the possibility of connecting with these non-religious, genderless energies.

2. Contemplative Exercises: Throughout the book, you'll find the Cerebrations designed to prompt reflection and contemplation. Engage with these thoughtfully, allowing the messages of the angels to permeate your consciousness. Journaling your thoughts and insights can deepen your connection with these celestial guides.

3. Daily Practices: Incorporate these Cerebrations into your daily routine. They are designed to help you maintain a connection with the angelic energies, creating a harmonious and supportive atmosphere in your life.

4. Mindfulness and Presence: Cultivate mindfulness and presence in your daily life. The angels communicate through subtle messages and signs, and being present allows you to perceive and interpret these messages more effectively.

5. Engage: Each day, as you embark on your journey through "Cerebrate!" you have the freedom to choose your path of contemplation. You can opt for spontaneity by randomly selecting a page, allowing the serendipity of the moment to guide your daily cerebration. Trust that the angels will lead you to the wisdom you need in that particular moment.

Alternatively, you may find guidance in the table of contents, offering a curated selection of topics aligned with your current needs or concerns. Allow your intuition to guide you as you let the angels direct your attention to the pages that hold messages most relevant to your life struggles or aspirations.

For those who prefer a systematic approach, moving from the beginning of the book to the end provides a structured and comprehensive journey. Sequentially exploring the chapters allows you to build a foundation of angelic understanding, gradually deepening your connection with these non-religious, genderless energies.

Whether you choose spontaneity, consult the table of contents, or follow the linear progression of the book, remember that each page holds a unique cerebration, a moment of thought crafted to resonate with the celestial energies surrounding you. Embrace the flexibility offered by this guide, allowing the angels to influence your daily reflections and lead you towards a life illuminated by their light and love.

As you delve into the pages of "Cerebrate!" may you find comfort, inspiration, and empowerment through your angels that surround you. Embrace the journey of self-discovery and transformation as you navigate life's challenges with the celestial support of these benevolent energies. In light and love, may you discover the profound impact of angelic guidance on your life's path.

We waste so much time and energy worrying about things that are out of our control.

I know I do...until...

I open myself to the angels - those beautiful, warrior energies who only want what's best for me.

And it's so easy...

"Angels, in light and love, calm me, reassure me, enlighten me, strengthen me and guide me on my transforming journey of healing. Thank you, Angels."

Activate Your Angels.

SECTION TWO

Meet Your Angels – An Overview of Each Angel

Archangel Michael, often depicted as a powerful warrior with a sword, is a prominent figure in various religious traditions, including Christianity, Judaism, and Islam. As the leader of the heavenly armies, Michael is believed to protect and defend against spiritual and physical threats, as well as guide souls towards righteousness and salvation. Known as the archangel of courage, strength, and justice, Michael is revered for his unwavering commitment to battling evil and promoting divine order. Many believers turn to him for protection, guidance, and assistance in times of need.

Archangel Gabriel, commonly depicted as a messenger with a trumpet, holds a significant role across multiple religious traditions, including Christianity, Judaism, and Islam. Often associated with communication, revelation, and divine guidance, Gabriel is believed to deliver important messages from God to humanity. In Christianity, Gabriel plays a pivotal role in announcing the birth of Jesus to Mary and foretelling other significant events. In Islam, Gabriel is known as Jibril and is regarded as the angel who revealed the Quran to the Prophet Muhammad. Gabriel's presence symbolizes hope, clarity, and divine intervention, and many believers seek his guidance and protection in times of uncertainty.

Archangel Raphael, known as the angel of healing, compassion, and guidance, holds a prominent place in various religious traditions, including Christianity, Judaism, and Islam. Often depicted with a staff and a fish, Raphael is believed to offer physical, emotional, and spiritual healing to those in need. In Christian tradition, Raphael is mentioned in the Book of Tobit, where he guides Tobias on a journey and heals his father's blindness. In Judaism, Raphael is also revered for his healing powers and his role in assisting individuals during times of trial. Whether seeking physical wellness, emotional solace, or spiritual renewal, believers often invoke Raphael's intercession for support and guidance along their journeys.

Archangel Uriel, is a revered figure in various religious traditions, including Christianity, Judaism, and esoteric belief systems. Often depicted carrying a book or a scroll, Uriel is associated with wisdom, enlightenment, and divine insight. In some traditions, Uriel is considered one of the seven archangels or one of the four cardinal archangels. While less prominent in mainstream texts, Uriel is believed to offer guidance, illumination, and understanding to those who seek spiritual enlightenment and truth. Devotees often turn to Uriel for assistance in matters of discernment, creativity, and intellectual pursuits.

Archangel Jophiel, is known for his association with beauty, creativity, and inner illumination. Often depicted with a flaming sword, Jophiel is believed to bring clarity, inspiration, and spiritual insight to those who seek guidance. While less prominent in mainstream religious texts, Jophiel is revered in esoteric and metaphysical traditions for his ability to help individuals perceive the beauty and goodness in all aspects of life, promoting inner peace and harmony. Devotees often invoke Jophiel's assistance to enhance their creativity, uplift their spirits, and cultivate a deeper appreciation for the wonders of existence.

Archangel Metatron, often depicted with a geometric cube or a fiery chariot, is a complex and multifaceted figure in mystical and esoteric traditions. Known as the angel of transformation, spiritual evolution, and sacred geometry, Metatron is believed to serve as a bridge between the divine and human realms. In some traditions, Metatron is considered one of the highest-ranking angels, with a direct connection to the divine throne. Metatron's presence is associated with spiritual growth, ascension, and the transmission of divine knowledge and wisdom. Devotees often seek Metatron's guidance and assistance in navigating personal and spiritual transformation, unlocking higher consciousness, and aligning with their true purpose.

Archangel Sandalphon, known as the angel of prayer and music, is revered for his role in facilitating communication between humans and the divine. Often depicted with a harp or a bow, Sandalphon is believed to help elevate prayers to the heavens and bring comfort to those who seek solace through music and spiritual devotion. In some traditions, Sandalphon is also associated with the earth and is considered the twin brother of Archangel Metatron. Devotees often turn to Sandalphon for assistance in deepening their connection to the divine, finding inner peace, and expressing their heartfelt prayers through music and creative expression.

Archangel Zadkiel, whose name means "Righteousness of God," is revered for his association with mercy, forgiveness, and spiritual transformation. Often depicted with a violet flame or wearing robes of deep blue or violet, Zadkiel is believed to help individuals release negative emotions, heal past traumas, and experience divine grace and forgiveness. In some traditions, Zadkiel is also considered the angel of memory, assisting in the recollection of important life lessons and guiding souls on their spiritual journeys. Devotees often invoke Zadkiel's intercession to transmute negativity into positivity, foster inner peace, and embrace forgiveness as a path to spiritual growth and enlightenment.

Archangel Haniel, is revered for her association with intuition, divine guidance, and the moon. Often depicted with lunar symbols or surrounded by celestial light, Haniel is believed to help individuals connect with their inner wisdom, intuition, and emotional intelligence. In some traditions, Haniel is also associated with love, fertility, and feminine power, guiding individuals in matters of relationships and self-expression. Devotees often turn to Haniel for assistance in enhancing their intuition, deepening their spiritual connections, and embracing their inner divine feminine energy.

Archangel Chamuel, is revered for his association with love, compassion, and inner peace. Often depicted with a pink ray of light or carrying a heart, Chamuel is believed to help individuals cultivate loving relationships, find inner harmony, and discover their life's purpose. In some traditions, Chamuel is also considered the angel of finding lost items and restoring harmony in relationships. Devotees often invoke Chamuel's assistance to heal emotional wounds, strengthen connections with others, and experience divine love and compassion in their lives.

Archangel Samuel, also known as Saint Samuel, is a figure in Abrahamic religions, particularly Judaism, Christianity, and Islam. He is considered a prophet and judge, known for anointing Saul as the first king of Israel. Samuel plays a crucial role in biblical narratives, including the call of the prophet Samuel, his guidance to King David, and his interactions with Saul. His life is celebrated in religious texts and commemorated in various religious practices and rituals. Samuel's story serves as an example of devotion to God and obedience to divine guidance, inspiring believers to seek spiritual insight and follow the path of righteousness.

Archangel Zachariel, also known as Sachiel, is revered for his association with abundance, prosperity, and spiritual expansion. Often depicted with symbols of wealth and abundance, such as a cornucopia or a golden chalice, Zachariel is believed to help individuals manifest their goals and desires, both material and spiritual. In some traditions, Zachariel is also associated with the planet Jupiter and its expansive energy, guiding individuals towards personal growth, wisdom, and generosity. Devotees often invoke Zachariel's assistance to attract abundance into their lives, expand their consciousness, and align with their highest purpose.

Archangel Laviah, also known as Laviel, is revered for his association with healing, protection, and spiritual growth. Although less well-known than some other archangels, Laviah is believed to offer comfort and solace to those in need, particularly during times of physical or emotional distress. Devotees often seek Laviah's intercession for healing, guidance, and support on their spiritual journeys. While specific attributes and associations may vary across different spiritual traditions, Laviah's presence is often invoked to bring peace, balance, and harmony into individuals' lives.

Archangel Jeremiel, also known as Ramiel, is revered for his association with prophecy, reflection, and divine guidance. Often depicted with a scroll or a book, Jeremiel is believed to assist individuals in reviewing their lives with compassion and understanding, offering insights and guidance for spiritual growth and transformation. In some traditions, Jeremiel is considered the angel of hope and helps individuals navigate through challenges by providing clarity and foresight. Devotees often turn to Jeremiel for assistance in understanding life's lessons, gaining perspective on past experiences, and finding hope and guidance for the future.

Archangel Raguel, is revered for his association with justice, harmony, and resolving conflicts. Often depicted holding a balance or scales, Raguel is believed to ensure fairness and order in the universe, promoting peace and reconciliation among individuals and groups. In some traditions, Raguel is considered the angel of justice and is invoked to bring about resolutions to disputes and injustices. Devotees often seek Raguel's intercession for guidance in resolving conflicts, restoring harmony in relationships, and promoting justice and fairness in their lives.

Archangel Raziel, is revered for his association with divine mysteries, wisdom, and esoteric knowledge. Often depicted with a large book or scroll, Raziel is believed to hold the keys to unlocking hidden truths and spiritual insights. In some traditions, Raziel is considered the angel of wisdom and is revered for his ability to impart knowledge and understanding to those who seek enlightenment. Devotees often turn to Raziel for guidance in uncovering the deeper meanings behind life's mysteries, accessing spiritual wisdom, and expanding their consciousness.

SECTION THREE

Daily Cerebrations – Calling Upon The Angels

Suffering can't be avoided. You can better deal with it, though, if you use your tools.

Yup...you've got suffering tools.

No...one of your tools is not curling up in a ball and sponsoring a pity party. Another is not wallowing in darkness and self-loathing. You see where I'm going with this...

Instead, get yourself geared up, fortified to withstand whatever life throws at you...because it can come fast and furious.

Use the tools that you've always had - your angels.

Your angels, always with you, bring you messages of guidance and support - constantly. You just need to be in regular contact with them, so that when you get hit with those life struggles 'bam' full on you're prepared to keep moving forward with your life.

These daily cerebrations give you a usable example of how you stay in daily contact with your angels. Talk to them - a lot.

Activate Your Angels.

RAPHAEL

Tangled webs can be compared to a lesson plan. If you look closely at a web while it appears tangled it's really quite organized although intricate. So, too, does a good lesson plan. Oftentimes it conveys the intent of what should be taught in addition to content. That's key. If we apply that to our Survivor Angels and our trauma we can move from the negative of our trauma to a healing space. I like Raphael for the instructor on this.

"Raphael, in your light and love show me how to identify my specific objectives, and my tasks with a realistic timeline to move me towards closure of my trauma. Thank you, Raphael."

Activate Your Angel.

Sadness....everybody experiences the sad emotion once in a while. When it's prolonged it needs attention. This is called 'taking care of yourself.' Acknowledge it AND know that it's okay to not feel okay. Stay connected. Don't go into hibernation. Being around others helps you to work through it even without talking about it. Raphael walks you through this, so let's go.

"Raphael, in light and love show me my joy in, and through, my sadness that I might burst forth from this melancholy. Thank you, Raphael."

Activate Your Angel.

Coping with family trauma can take on many behaviors. Everything from people-pleasing to constant comparison with others to relationship issues to physical and mental disorders to feelings of guilt. The list goes on.

This is one of those areas where you need professional help as your coping skills along with those experiences that caused the family trauma impact your brain. This is nothing to take lightly.

In the meantime though, Raphael can bring you comfort.

"Raphael I know that my personality was shaped by negative childhood situations. I need you to stay by my side to give me courage and strength to seek the professional assistance that I need. Thank you, Raphael."

Activate Your Angel.

Angels are telling me that we all need to revisit some grounding or earthing, as some call it. It's been a long Winter and it's not over yet.

I love grounding because it's soothing, it's relaxing, it calms the anxiety, stress, and overwhelming feelings. It brings you back to your center.

It also reduces inflammation, decreases pain, and improves your sleep.

Raphael brings the calm.

"Raphael, in light and love, connect me to Mother Earth so that I feel the discharge of static drain away. Help me to find the technique right for me, and then motivate me to stay with it. I want to feel my blood flowing with ease as I continue this practice to promote better mental and physical health. Thank you, Raphael."

Activate Your Angel.

HANIEL

Put your positive pants on. You heard me. Put your positive pants on. It's so much more than your attitude. It's changing your perspective. It's not taking things personally. It's being happy for others' success. Wearing your positive pants lowers your negative levels, meaning it lowers your pain and distress (mentally), not to mention giving you physical resistance to illness. I think we should invite Haniel to help us with this.

"Haniel, in light and love open me to humor, laughter, gratitude, and spending time with positive people. I'm ready to get dressed - positively. Thank you, Haniel."

Activate Your Angels.

I practiced quiet emotions for years. Quiet emotions are when you silently harbor them.

Trauma survivors learn to do this when no one helps them with their emotions as a child.

It's a tough practice to stop. It's necessary though to stop the practice. If you don't you will struggle all of your life with unexpressed emotions.

We could call on Chamuel. Instead we're going to call on Haniel.

"Haniel, in light and love, bring to the surface all of the emotions that lie buried deep within me. In light and love, show me how to do this in measured steps with the goal of purging myself of the negativity this has caused, and bring balance. Thank you, Haniel."

Activate Your Angel.

Some lessons we just learn too late in life. It's true for everyone. Some of the lessons can slide in the grand scheme of things.

Are there some, though, that we really should pay more attention to?

The biggest one given our world culture seems to be 'your happiness is your own choice and your own doing.' It's a self-realization factor that can make or break your overall life.

Haniel brings messages that direct you in putting your life in perspective.

"Haniel, in light and love, I need your thoughts to help me find balance and harmony. I'm tired of the frustration and disappointment. Thank you, Haniel."

Activate Your Angel.

MICHAEL

Danger is real...Fear is a choice. You've survived trauma. You can move forward without that fear. You learned from your experience. You learned the warning signs. You can now step out, tackling your triggers to find they are no longer things to be feared. Let's call on Michael.

"Michael, I need you to help me in light and love to conquer my trigger fears so that I can continue my survival journey. Thank you, Michael."

Activate Your Angel.

Irritability. How crabby are you? How often are you crabby? Trauma survivors often feel on edge, keyed-up...irritable. It's because trauma makes you feel unsafe. It's because for a moment you weren't in control. Every little thing will set you off. It's time to feel the control that you innately have. Michael heals us internally through his communicative powers.

"Michael, the ultimate communication healing you can share is needed to show me, in light and love, how and where control still resides within me. Thank you, Michael, for restoring my inner peace."

Activate Your Angel.

Hyper focused...hyper vigilant...hyper aroused...all possible side effects of trauma. Hyper means to be highly whatever, so highly focused, highly vigilant or highly aroused...up a level from the usual. It can be exhausting. It can also be isolating because you avoid situations that prompt these actions. Know that Michael stands ready to keep you at the lower level whenever you need him.

"Michael, in light and love, as protector of my inner communications, bring me back to a place of calm whenever I feel myself moving into hyper mood. Thank you, Michael."

Activate Your Angel.

So many times when you're a trauma survivor you feel powerless. Fear overrides any feelings of self-worth.

Powerlessness means that you believe that you lack the control over factors or events that affect you. It's a mental state. You can overcome this.

The first step begins with recognizing that you are no longer a victim. You are a survivor. Whatever happened to you is over, which removes victim status. Your mindset of remaining a victim is voluntary. You've chosen it. Michael strengthens us and gives us courage to release us from those voluntary fears and doubts of our self-worth.

"Michael, in light and love, I need you to help me take back control of my life...to develop my core self, to give me courage to speak up for myself, and align myself with the flow of positive personal growth. Thank you, Michael, for your never-ending support."

Activate Your Angel.

Value your life and you'll value all life.

Many lost that somewhere along the way. Humanity, though, never forgot that.

When you value yourself, you value others. It really is that simple - if you don't let all of the distractions get in the way.

Through your struggles you want to believe that you have value. But no matter what has happened to you - YOU HAVE VALUE.

Michael leads the self-esteem charge because it is that important.

"Michael, in light and love remind me of my value. Then show me how to project that value onto others that they see theirs as well. I really want this world to be a better place for all. Thank you, Michael."

Activate Your Angel.

This one will hit home for just about everybody. Phubbing.

Phubbing is 'the practice of ignoring one's companion or companions in order to pay attention to one's phone or other mobile device.' Yes, there is such a syndrome - Phubbing.

It falls under isolation or abandonment when done constantly or to extreme. Phubbing causes trauma for those companions.

Michael can sort out this technological malady.

"Michael, as a great communicator, I need you to step in and tell me how to overcome this traumatic behavior that I experience from others. In light and love guide me to open their eyes and let my feelings be known. Thank you, Michael."

Activate Your Angel.

Consistency leads to habit. Engaging yourself in positive activities regularly soon leads to healthy habits.

This is crucial to your healing journey.

For motivation and encouragement, because this is so important, you want Michael.

"In light and love, Michael, please keep giving me the nudges that keep me on a consistent, steady path using positive energy to succeed with my wellness plan. Thank you, Michael."

Activate Your Angel.

GABRIEL

Depression busting starts with getting up early. Lingering in bed might seem like a 'safe' thing to do. In reality it only compounds your mental state. Just getting out of bed is physical activity and if you cook for yourself, go for a walk, clean a room, it starts releasing endorphins. Also, avoid sleeping during the day and don't overindulge in caffeine or alcohol. Gabriel motivates even the most sluggish earthlings.

"Gabriel, in light and love, get me up and at 'em...every day. Get me moving. Get me energized. Get me motivated. Thank you, Gabriel...let's go for a walk."

Activate Your Angel.

Summer time. Summer time. Sum Sum Summer time.

A mom's busiest season usually. But there's also school breaks. It's not limited just to Summer.

Kids might be out of school, but there's camps, and retreats, and sports, and theatre, family getaways, and the list goes on. Plus when the kids aren't running off somewhere you need to figure out how to keep them entertained.

Stop! Stop entertaining them. Let them figure it out themselves.

Gabriel becomes your best friend in the Summer.

"Gabriel, in light and love, help me to stop hovering and cajoling and entertaining my kids so that they can find their creative and self-sufficient sides. Thank you, Gabriel."

Activate Your Angel.

I was thinking the other day, how cool would it be if there was an angel walk-up window?

You just step up and place your order when the angel greets you.

That's really how it works with the angels. You simply step up to them in your heart and mind and put in your order.

Now your order must include very specific requests so that your intention is clear.

Gabriel can help you communicate your order.

"Gabriel, I'm working on this whole angel communication thing. So, in light and love, send me some messages as to how I can most effectively make my requests. Thank you, Gabriel."

Activate Your Angel.

Your essence or your truest self. Sometimes it takes years to realize your essence.

It doesn't leave you, but it can get muddled by societal impacts, relationship effects and traumatic experiences. You may have a dream about someone. It's probably not what they look like that you're dreaming about but rather who they are as a person. We have feelings when we're in the presence of others.

It's the same for us. We have feelings when we stray from our essence and when we return to it. Moving away from it will bring darker emotions while moving closer will bring more positive emotions.

Gabriel delves deep into messages.

"Gabriel, in light and love, message me about my essence. Through creative expression help me to recognize new outputs and sources that connect me back with my true essence. Thank you, Gabriel."

Activate Your Angel.

Imagination can assist with trauma healing. Since trauma is a human reality for just about everyone at some point in their life, and imagination is embedded in us, it's a natural connection for healing.

This connection really isn't a new method for healing. It goes back as far as 1491 to Spain and St Ignatius. No stranger to trauma, Ignatius developed Spiritual Exercises to cope with his trauma. Those exercises are applicable today.

Gabriel provides the right 'links' to use these exercises.

"Gabriel, in light and love, show me how to daily employ the components of Ignatius' exercises, namely focusing on a place, contemplating its life-giving attributes, then expressing the feelings, ideas, fears or hopes that come to mind. Thank you, Gabriel."

Activate Your Angel.

Soulless. What does it mean to be soulless?

Our souls are our essence. Our souls are our very being. So, what does this mean?

It means that one lacks human qualities and the ability to feel or produce deep feelings. Some synonyms include ruthless, heartless, inhuman, oppressive and merciless. Those are words that you might use to describe those who caused your trauma.

What that should tell you is that you share no blame in what happened to you. You can put any guilt aside, as this was not invited, welcomed or considered.

Gabriel eases the negative surrounding this.

"Gabriel, I've survived my trauma but I am still haunted with guilt that I might have had a hand in causing it. In light and love, show me how to overcome this untruth. Thank you, Gabriel."

Activate Your Angel.

Others' success. Wearing your positive pants lowers your negative levels, meaning it lowers your pain and distress (mentally) not to mention giving you physical resistance to illness. I think we should invite Haniel to help us on this.

CHAMUEL

Treat your best friend...YOU are your own best friend. No one is going to treat you better than you treat yourself. Take time for you. Make time for you. Make one special gift for yourself every day...even if it's a momentary pep talk, or a quick self-hug. You are worth every second of whatever you do for yourself. Chamuel loves to butter you up.

"Chamuel, shower me with light and love so I can shower myself with love. Thank you, Chamuel."

Activate Your Angel.

Rain chatter...the rhythm of the rain. I love it. That wonderful chatter helps lull the brain into sleep mode by blocking noise, which relaxes you. Everyone perceives rain sounds to be non-threatening, so for trauma survivors it's a perfect sleeping pill. While similar to white noise it's considered pink noise, so with Chamuel's aura being pink, I know he's so ready to help with your lullaby.

"Chamuel, as I find rain chatter to listen to I ask you in light and love to rock me into a calming and restoring slumber. Thank you, Chamuel."

Activate Your Angel.

Chill. Something that we're all familiar with in the Winter as we shiver through these seemingly unending months. In this case though, you should 'chill' from any unnecessary demands. Allow yourself to slow down, taking time to notice the world around you, the people around you, and the vibe around you. Let Chamuel help you find what you're looking for in the new year.

"Chamuel, in light and love shower me with your peace that I might focus on the direction for my life. Thank you, Chamuel."

Activate Your Angel.

Anxiety during the holidays, all holidays, probably takes center stage for you. Anxiety after a holiday generally is a combination of fatigue, unmet expectations, and the anticipation of the next one. Fear not. They're survivable.

You can indulge in massage therapy, practice journaling, try acupuncture, get some sleep, enjoy oil diffusers and essential oils - the main thing boils down to taking care of yourself. Chamuel loves to pamper.

"Chamuel, in light and love please just 'sit' with me. I need to calm my anxiety-ridden self to remove holiday residual. Thank you, Chamuel, for easing me through this time."

Activate Your Angel.

AI... Artificial Intelligence. It's been around awhile.

The concern that I have with AI involves the human factor. To date they can't replicate feelings and emotions.

Feelings and emotions don't exist with AI. That's a problem for everyone.

Feelings and emotions are necessary to know empathy and sympathy and sadness and love and joy and peace. Without feelings and emotions we're just walking zombies. We lose all reason for life.

Chamuel stands front and center in circumventing the loss of our humanity.

"Chamuel, in light and love, shine a beacon on retaining and expanding what makes us human. I need this to understand my purpose, my healing, and how I fit into this world. Thank you, Chamuel."

Activate Your Angel.

Kenny Chesney's song, "There Goes My Life" speaks to what it means to lose your life to someone else.

Parents often feel like they lose their life when their children come into this world. What they find out, though, is that they *find* their life...in loving their children.

Being a parent helps teach us how to look outside of ourselves. It teaches us how to give of ourselves. It teaches us how to sacrifice and in return receive something even more valuable.

Chamuel lights the way for losing one's life.

"Chamuel, I know that one of the important pieces of trauma healing comes when I lose myself to others; when I stop obsessing with my own life; and realize the effect that I'm having on those around me. In light and love, guide me in healthy ways to lose my life in order to gain my life. Thank you, Chamuel."

Activate Your Angel.

It's possible that a part of your brain triggers out-of-body experiences, according to scientists.

They've known for some time that certain drugs (ketamine for one) and electricity pulses can do this also.

The location is toward the front of the brain called the anterior precuneus. When 'poked' it changes our sense of physical self. It's what tells us that something is happening to us - not someone else.

The brain gets confused as the inner ear may be saying that you're moving yet our eyes say otherwise. To compensate the brain goes on a journey outside of us. The take away from this is that this might aid in depression.

Chamuel, in addition to other archangels, communicates to you your best path forward.

"Chamuel, it's not that I want an out-of-body experience, however I need to sort out my realities. So, in light and love stimulate the area of my brain through your messages to accomplish this. Thank you, Chamuel."

Activate Your Angel.

Clutter creates chaos. Decluttering eliminates chaos.

It gets tough to focus when you're trying to locate things. You also get brain fog because your brain hits overload. You definitely won't remember where you put something that you're looking for and anything else.

Excessive clutter leads to negative feelings. Excessive clutter affects your sleep. Excessive clutter makes you "Donna/Donald Downer".

Chamuel loves to declutter.

"Chamuel, I'm buried in a mountain of 'stuff' physically and therefore mentally. In light and love, help me start with baby steps, even asking for help to part with unnecessary and unwanted items. Then show me fulfilling sources to donate my belongings. Thank you, Chamuel."

Activate Your Angel.

Self-compassion simply means being kind to yourself. The components include self-kindness, common humanity and mindfulness.

Rather than tying this to trauma survivors, though, who know they have difficulties with this, which roots itself in self-love as a result of trauma - I'm directing this at those who interact with trauma survivors. Compassion is necessary for all of humanity to survive.

As those on the outside of others' trauma you need to recognize their suffering and feel moved by it. That doesn't mean that you feel sorry for them. It means that you don't judge them...you don't criticize them. You just need to be present for them. Listen. Really listen.

To accomplish this you must first practice self compassion for you. Accept your humanness.

Chamuel shines the light on this endeavor.

"Chamuel, in light and love please clear my mind clutter so that I can focus on others. Help me to stop mentally beating myself up. Then I can shift my focus to this need in my presence. Thank you, Chamuel."

Activate Your Angel.

ZADKIEL

Brave...courageous....adjectives that friends and families call or called you as a trauma survivor. Hmmmmm.......You're just not feeling it though. Angels have probably been telling you that you need to change that thinking. Hmmmmmm.....you've been ignoring them. Yes, the trauma was frightening. Yes, the trauma seemed unending. It's over though, and you survived. You might still have work to do, but you're braver than you think. It's time to get Zadkiel amped up.

"Zadkiel, my courage link needs some encouragement, so in light and love I'd love it if you would give me that boost to find the counselor/ therapist that's just right for me. Thank you, Zadkiel."

Activate Your Angel.

Write a new story today. Wait...But you say that you have writer's block. Writer's block is merely a temporary impasse. You just need to know how to break the block. Like with writer's block, trauma can be overcome. You're already a survivor, so now you just have to think of all the good things that can come next. Zadkiel can give you all of the tools that you need.

"Zadkiel, I feel like I'm locked up...stuck in a rut...unable to write a new story today. In light and love, help me to set a double-goal that I might accomplish one, and support me when I'm not quite hitting the mark, but I'm trying. Thank you, Zadkiel."

Activate Your Angel.

Self-esteem refers to a positive subjective view of self-worth. Narcissism, on the other hand, holds feelings of superiority and self-entitlement.

Self-esteem and Narcissism do possess certain common elements. One is positive self-perceptions. That's pretty much where it ends though, as Narcissists do not have high self-esteem.

Narcissism can be a result of trauma obtained through abuse, especially emotional and mental abuse. Even from parents who base their acceptance on unrealistic outcomes rather than who the child is.

Narcissists may experience hyperarousal when exposed to different forms of social judgement. This could also happen with those who possess high self-esteem. The difference, though, is the narcissist won't have the tools to cope.

Zadkiel assists narcissists and abuse survivors to untangle the limiting thoughts.

"Zadkiel, I know that I crave approval and acceptance at every turn. In light and love bring me to a level of good self-esteem so that I might feel value, acceptance and love regardless of my actions or words. Thank you, Zadkiel."

Activate Your Angel.

SANDALPHON

"Sing...Sing a song....Sing out loud...Sing out strong. Sing of good things, not bad...Sing of happy, not sad." (By Joseph Raposo)

Music in and of itself uses every nook and cranny of our minds. It's the best mental exercise there is. So, sing.....even if you're not a singer. Open up everything. Open your ears, your throat, your diaphragm, your mind.....your voice. Release it all. Free yourself...free your mind. Sandolphon loves to liberate with music

"Sandolphon, let's bring light and love into my mind, singing together loud and strong to brighten my life and those around me. Thank you, Sandolphon."

Activate Your Angel.

Sun dogs, more visible in Winter, are members of the halo family. They appear from the refraction of sunlight by ice crystals in the air. They can be seen anywhere in the world during any season; however, their brightness will be affected given the sun's position.

I love sun dogs as they remind me of Angels. Those halos tell me that Angels are near. Sandalphon can help you get the most of your sun dog experience.

"Sandalphon, your attunement with nature tells me that you can highlight my sun dog watching. In light and love show me how to recognize your message in those beautiful creations. Thank you, Sandalphon."

Activate Your Angel.

Trees hold healing powers. Because of their meditative state they use a very subtle energy form to communicate.

In addition to converting carbon dioxide to oxygen, trees also take in negative vibes and return them as positive energy.

The deeper and higher they go, the more spiritual they become. They live side by side with us and all of nature, helping to maintain balance in the world.

Sandalphon shows us how we can use our trees' healing powers for our greater good.

"Sandalphon, in light and love, whisper to me through the rustling of the tree leaves the healing messages that balance and ground me. Thank you, Sandalphon."

Activate Your Angel.

Angels communicate through music.

Name one person who doesn't like some form of music...has a favorite song...a piece that 'moves' them more than anything else on this earth.

Music truly embodies a universal language. It's unifying. All of our emotions unite in music and move us to 'feel'...to be alive. Those feelings that we experience through music are messages from our Angels.

Sandalphon would be the Archangel primarily responsible. This might seem a bit odd considering Sandalphon oversees nature. But think about that...

"Sandalphon, your messages of harmony, and synchronicity with nature find the perfect medium in music. In light and love, shower me with the melodies and symphonies that I need in all moments of my life to feel alive and move me to gratitude. Thank you, Sandalphon."

Activate Your Angel.

All of our lives are individual stories. That's why I love talking to people.

What we all forget in our story though, is that sometimes we hit setbacks. Issues resurface.

It's okay. Life is a dance...not an on/off event.

Sandalphon helps choreograph your dance.

"Sandalphon, in light and love, help me to hear your teaching/leading steps as I continually ground myself and overcome setbacks. Thank you, Sandalphon."

Activate Your Angel.

Scientists have discovered an 'unusual cardiovascular response when people listen to classical music together'.

People come together. They synchronize. Their breathing, heartrate and even their skin electricity become one.

I'm not surprised at all. Classical music embraces the entire brain, feeding it with positive growth. It's one reason why professionals encourage playing classical music for infants and children.

As adults we need it even more. Social media, news media and other outside influences have separated our collectiveness. It's led to many life struggles.

Sandalphon can bring you to this beautiful music to ease that stress.

"Sandalphon, in light and love, prompt me to gather with others and experience the life changing benefits from the gift of classical music. I want to be part of bringing our hurting world together. Thank you, Sandalphon."

Activate Your Angel.

METATRON

'I want to fly like an eagle, to the sea, Fly like an eagle, let my spirit carry me. I want to fly like an eagle Fly right into the future.' Great song. [written by Steve Miller]

As trauma survivors we can visualize those lyrics because that's what we long for. Well, long no more. I think you should solicit some flight tips from Metatron.

"Metatron, you're all about taking us to new heights. In light and love I'd like to soar with you to light activated positivity. Thank you, Metatron."

Activate Your Angel.

'Time keeps on turnin, turnin, into the future.' (An old mid-century tune that I love.)

Time stops for no one, nor does it slow down, so we need to make the most of the time that we have. If you're haunted by trauma, time can be a good thing. Time keeps you moving...forward. The past is the past. The present is the present and the future remains to be seen. You possess endless possibilities for making your future a thing of renewal and healing. Metatron works wonders when it comes to time and renewal.

"Metatron, in light and love I'm looking to the future to regain control of my life that I might make plans to heal from my past, and experience a fulfilled life. Your guidance and support will see me through to say 'Hello, Tomorrow'. Thank you, Metatron."

Activate Your Angel.

JOPHIEL

Music and the brain - a remarkable pairing. It's the only pairing that involves the entire brain. You can sing, play an instrument, drum or simply listen to music. It's all about synchronizing your heart and your mind. Brain wave entertainment involves the frequencies of sound. It's a little geeky, but interesting to try if you're looking for something a little different. Jophiel brings you hours of delight through the arts, and will help your musical selection.

"Jophiel, in light and love conduct an orchestra in my heart and mind through the sound of music that will synchronize and balance my positivity. Thank you, Jophiel."

Activate Your Angel.

Confirmation bias: The tendency to interpret new information by looking for or interpreting information that confirms one's existing beliefs. It ignores inconsistent information. Oftentimes life struggles are a direct result of confirmation bias. Some would call it closed mindedness. When it starts affecting your daily life and health it's time to call in the angels. Open your mind to solicit the assistance of Jophiel.

"Jophiel, I need you to open my mind in light to love to seek and receive opposing viewpoints and different information sources that I might make balanced decisions and life choices to improve myself and the world. Thank you, Jophiel."

Activate Your Angel.

Prince... "dearly beloved, we are gathered here today to get through this thing called life."

We sure are.

Life isn't black and white. It's beautiful HD colors with all of the shades and hues and complexities. Gorgeous. Amazing. Overwhelming for some. That's okay. It's not insurmountable. Jophiel organizes your thought processes to deal with shades and hues.

"Jophiel, every day there's something that tries to shut me down. In light and love please bring clarity and organization to the things that overwhelm and keep me from relishing life. Thank you, Jophiel."

Activate Your Angel.

Listening deeply means we go beyond what the person is saying. We listen for what's behind their feelings, and what do they actually want. That's what we need to do with our own words and thoughts. We need to start deeply listening to what our mind is projecting and re-direct the negative pieces. Jophiel provides great mind balance.

"Jophiel, some balance is needed in my mind to help me realize what is constructive and what is destructive. Help me to listen attentively and deeply to keep me moving in light and love on my healing journey. Thank you, Jophiel."

Activate Your Angel.

Peace loading. I saw this recently:

Peace is accepting today, releasing yesterday, and giving up the need to control tomorrow. As trauma survivors we need to visit this every day. Peace, you see, doesn't come from religion. It comes from our soul and our soul is pure energy. Jophiel guides us there.

"Jophiel, I know that peace is a gift that I can receive, because it comes from within me. In light and love I await your guidance down the path to inner peace. Thank you, Jophiel."

Activate Your Angel.

I love sticky buns. A sticky mind is another thing.

But what is a sticky mind? First of all, it can be a little elusive. It also can run in families where a parent struggles with it. Finally, it's basically when you get so bogged down worrying that you start making up the end game.

If you're already dealing with anything chronic, conflict, and/or stress it makes you see yourself as an anxious person. You don't always realize that it doesn't have to lead to torment. It is NOT mental illness.

Jophiel steps up to help you redirect those thoughts.

"Jophiel, I'm a worry wart. Sometimes it even consumes me. In light and love, help to know the true alarm bells from the false. Thank you, Jophiel."

Activate Your Angel.

Trauma makes our world feel like it's out of control. It doesn't have to.

We control almost our entire life. We have free will, so we can pick and choose, add and delete, stay and go.

We just need to listen to our angels to help us make those decisions.

"Jophiel, in light and love, coach me with your messages to regain control of my life. I know that if I follow your positive guidance I can do this. Thank you, Jophiel."

Activate Your Angel.

JEREMIEL

Nature's creatures show us such an instinctive way to survive. You simply move. They know when and where to make their move and it seems effortless.

Autumn provides us a beautiful backdrop to this movement. Just step outside and look to the skies. Thousands upon thousands of birds sail across the Fall sky on their semi-annual migration. Our migration back to positivity doesn't come quite as easily. Let's invite Jeremiel in to keep us on track for our journey.

"Jeremiel, in light and love, point me towards the 'up' side of life so that I might take flight on the better side of life. And when you see me starting to U-turn, correct my journey to keep my face in the sun. Thank you, Jeremiel."

Activate Your Angel.

Blather. Blather. Blather. Blathering...such an odd word. It's nonsensical talking or writing. As trauma survivors we often feel like everything we hear and read about 'us' is just blathering. Some might call it cognitive dissonance because we don't believe anyone else understands us. The truth is, though, that you're not alone. Others do understand - maybe not exactly but a common thread exists. It's us who need to open the door even if it's just a crack to start, and begin trusting others. Jeremiel takes center stage in healing our emotions and thoughts.

"Jeremiel, in light and love please give me the support that I need to crack open that door, to allow others to peek in and help me heal. Thank you, Jeremiel, for having my back."

Activate Your Angel.

Falling leaves and color change. Change. So easy for trees. Change for us is a lifetime exercise, too. Exercise means work. We'd rather settle for short-term gratification and worry about the rest later. It also means commitment, a fading value. So, to overcome life struggles you've got to go public. Jeremiel doesn't settle for the short-term. He's in it for the long haul.

"Jeremiel, in light and love, please keep me uplifted, motivated, energized, and optimistic to pursue the changes that I need to be a valuable contributor to this world. Thank you, Jeremiel."

Activate Your Angel.

Emotional numbing means that someone is unable to experience emotions. Temporary numbing might not be bad, but when it's extended it's because you're building a wall to protect yourself from any more physical or emotional pain. This is often a result of trauma that can have long-term consequences. Jeremiel heals our emotions, so let's bring him in on this.

"Jeremiel, in light and love, I need you to bring closure to the painful emotions that prevent me from feeling any emotion. I want to 'feel' again. Thank you, Jeremiel."

Activate Your Angel.

Numbness can be a coping mechanism. But if it gets to emotional blunting, you run the risk of physical decline. You need to feel the full range of emotions in order to express emotions. Physical symptoms include but are not limited to restlessness, difficulty speaking, and forgetfulness. Jeremiel possesses in-depth knowledge for healing your emotions.

"Jeremiel, I think that my emotions took a hiatus to the point of affecting my health. In light and love, I need you to remove the numbness and restore the appropriate level of feelings that I need to protect myself overall. Thank you, Jeremiel."

Activate Your Angel.

Aching...feeling old?

Everybody deals with aging. We just deal with it differently...maybe.

The key to embracing the aging process, which can't be avoided, involves your 'inner' eye. We must look to the future as we learn from the past. Then we must be in the moment...present...and keep a sense of humor...and dream about what still can come. After all, we're still here.

Jeremiel loves a good planning process.

"Jeremiel, in light and love show me the possibilities to still experience adventures even though they might look different from a few years ago. I know that nothing is set in stone, so let's go find some new opportunities. Thank you, Jeremiel."

Activate Your Angel.

Mindfulness builds belonging when it focuses on the here and now. That is amplified when done with curiosity and acceptance.

This tells us that it's more than just a wellness technique.

What was once practiced only by those cloistered in monasteries, mindfulness transcends the majority of us around the world. This provides a strong sense of belonging.

Noticing our thoughts and emotions, taking deep breaths and just plain slowing down frees us to look outward and feel 'one' with others.

Jeremiel is ideal for guiding you further.

"Jeremiel, in light and love, show me how much I've already opened myself to the world and how I can continue to enlighten myself for further healing. Thank you, Jeremiel."

Activate Your Angel.

URIEL

Today's gift - TODAY! Yes, your gift today is TODAY! Sounds too easy, but there it is all the same. Every day is a gift. Good days. Bad days. They're all a gift. On good days we relish the positive vibes. On bad days we assess what happened, learn from it, and move on...or we should. That learning piece is a huge gift that we often overlook especially as trauma survivors. We just see the dark side of the day and miss the ray of sunshine that is also there. Uriel shows us those rays of sunshine.

"Uriel, you possess the infinite gift of illuminating our daily gifts. In light and love, every day, show me the gifts of the day that otherwise I would miss. Thank you, Uriel."

Activate Your Angel.

Psychologists tell us that labeling each other such as musician, jock, nerd, etc. might reflect who someone is at that moment, but it also carries a belief that that's who they innately are. That says they can't change. It's dangerous then because people can and do change. When it comes to trauma survivors, change, while scary, helps you evolve into a healthier person. It then becomes necessary to ignore any labels that others and you might be hanging on you. Uriel detoxifies just these type of thoughts.

"Uriel, I need you to flush the labels out of my life, in light and love. I need you to replace those labels with positive expressions of thankfulness for myself. Thank you, Uriel."

Activate Your Angel.

Wednesday is popularly known as hump day, a phrase coined by Roy Mann in the early 1960's around a water cooler.

It characterizes the supposed drudgery of the work week.

Many struggle with work in general not realizing that it's part of our soul contract.

"Uriel, in light and love, carry me through my work week in positivity and with a renewed sense of purpose. Thank you, Uriel."

Activate Your Angel.

Emotion is part of your soul. When your emotions suffer it affects all of you. Emotional harvest then means you take the time to gather your emotions so you can assess and learn from them. Trauma emotions create patterns that are so strong you can only process them after they happen. Shamanic, Celtic and other traditions start the harvest by drawing a circle around you. It becomes a sacred space and connects you with the Spirit of the source, and starts the restoration of your soul. Uriel will guide you through the rest.

"Uriel, show me my connection to my future to the front of me; the guardian of my past behind me; guardian of my intuition to my left; guardian of my strategic mind to my right; the sky for a motherly protection from above; the earth for a motherly protection from below; and my heart for the love that surrounds me and resides within. (Now, check how you feel.) Thank you, Uriel."

Activate Your Angel.

Stress doesn't come from your relationships, your job, your boss, your life choices.

It comes from what and how you think about them.

Uriel can help you shift that perspective.

"Uriel, in light and love, help me to start redirecting my stress response from my emotions to my thought process. I want to shift my stress perspective and learn to minimize the feelings that defeat me. Thank you, Uriel."

Activate Your Angel.

RAGUEL

Knock knock.

Who's there?

Your angel.

Hahahahaha...or not. Knock knock jokes originated before 1936 in several Midwest locations...as far as anyone knows. Their popularity spread across America, over to Europe, and beyond. The funny puns eventually rubbed some the wrong way so were banned in the U.S. for a bit.

I picked this particular one because your angels continuously knock on your life. They've sent you so many messages to bring you light and love you should be blinded by the light. So, it is time to open you up to those wonderful messengers. Oh, Raguel, your magic is needed.

"Raguel, this can wait no longer. I need you to break down any walls that prevent me from receiving my Angel messages. In light and love, please fill me with those calming and uplifting angel frequencies. Thank you, Raguel."

Activate Your Angel.

Would you rather be alone all your life or be surrounded by really annoying people? That's an incredibly valid question if you struggle through your days, as you do have options. There is value in spending time alone AND there is value socializing even if people can be annoying. A lot of times people come off as annoying because of your current mood. So before you toss them to the side and retreat to the quieter side call on Raguel help sort it out.

"Raguel, I'm pondering my situation concerning my mood and perception of those around me. In light and love please bring me clarity that I might restore harmony within myself and with others. Thank you. Raguel."

Activate Your Angel.

Attunement is a lost art. But it can facilitate healing for many...especially trauma survivors.

When you attune to someone you make them feel like they're the center of your attention. This can be terrifying as all of a sudden their needs come bubbling to the surface and you may feel unsafe. The good news is that you don't need to meet those needs - just validate them.

Raguel attunes with the best of them.

"Raguel, in light and love, talk me through how to be present, eliminating distractions, even in the hard conversations so that both of us gradually feel safer in our relationship and expand our capacities for consistent attunement. Thank you, Raguel."

Activate Your Angel.

LAVIAH

Warriors! Angels are warriors.

Don't think of them as the cute little cherubs or the beautiful winged gods and goddesses. Angels aren't even close to that.

They do exude and work in light and love. It's a light and love that means to ensure that you receive your messages come 'hell or high water' though. Don't take them for granted.

Laviah reveals their true gifts.

"Laviah, in light and love, show me the 'tough' warrior love that my angels carry to help me in my life. That way I can more effectively call upon them to guide and direct my thoughts and actions. Thank you, Laviah."

Activate Your Angel.

SECTION FOUR

MULTIPLE ANGELS

The difference between being grateful and being thankful boils down to this: Being grateful is an action while being thankful is a feeling. Given this clarification, that makes feeling thankful personal...it's about how you feel. As you struggle, identifying the things that make you feel thankful provide healing moments in your journey. If you can also express 'gratefulness' of your identified blessings you're creating another layer of 'good.' Azrael, Zadkiel, and Raziel provide guidance to move you in this direction.

"Azrael, Zadkeil, and Raziel, I call on you in light and love to point me to those things in my life that I am thankful for. Then I can express my gratitude to those who got me there and/or for the things that I've been taking for granted. I know that those things exist in my life. Thank you, Azrael, Zadkiel, and Raziel."

Now Activate Your Angels!

Trauma bonding, while not unusual, stymies your healing journey. This occurs, generally, in cases of abuse where the trauma survivor forms an attachment to the abuser sometimes without realizing it. Because abuse is more than a one-and-done event this bond intentionally needs to be broken. This tie is generally quite strong so it will require Chamuel, Raphael, Jophiel and Jeremiel's intervention.

"Chamuel, Raphael, Jophiel and Jeremiel, in light and love I call you in to sever the emotionally bonding tie to my abuser so that I might breathe freely again. Thank you Chamuel, Raphael, Jophiel and Jeremiel."

Activate Your Angels.

Campfires evoke an incredible sense of peace. It's mesmerizing to sit in the chill night air, gazing into the flames, listening to the crackling of the wood, smelling that smokiness, and basking in the warmth like a blanket wrapped around you. Your angels, Michael and Jophiel, stand ready for a fireside chat with you.

"Michael and Jophiel, please join me around the campfire to illuminate the peace within and around me, in light and love. You're assigned to bring the marshmallows...I've got the rest covered. Thank you, Michael and Jophiel."

Activate Your Angels.

Risky behavior provides therapists key evidence of PTSD in trauma survivors. It can take the form of excessive drinking, going into dangerous situations or areas, or hanging out with people who are negative and unhealthy for you. This depth of trauma survival requires professional intervention which comes in multiple forms. Michael and Zadkiel will work with you to get you the intervention right for you.

"Michael and Zadkiel, I know that I'm doing myself no favors with my behavior. In light and love, I welcome you to show me the danger I'm about to put myself in and protect me from me. Then, guide me to the help that will heal me. Thank you, Michael and Zadkiel."

Activate Your Angels.

Having witnessed hurricanes like Ian and Fiona it's hard to imagine anything peaceful about these large magnitude storms. Trauma leaves us feeling the same way...asking "when will our storm subside?" In the eye of the storm, though, it's as peaceful as the outside is devastating. You just need to fight your way to that center to find the peace. Raphael, Jophiel and Chamuel combine forces to help get you there.

"Raphael, Jophiel, and Chamuel, please give me the strength and guidance to bring myself to my center. I need to bring peace to my turmoil that engulfs me like a storm. In light and love, I invite you in. Thank you, Raphael, Jophiel and Chamuel."

Activate Your Angels.

Snow. I love it. Maybe it's because I grew up in the Midwest with snow up to my eyeballs. Or maybe because it's fascinating. When it snows there are billions upon gazillions of snowflakes falling and no two are the same. Imagine that. Sit with that. No two trauma survivors are the same, either. That's why Survivor Angels tries to come at this from all different angles and perspectives. Chamuel and Raphael join forces to assist all of you on this.

"Chamuel and Raphael, I know that timing is everything and that my healing time looks different from everyone else's. I also know that in light and love you come in and guide me, allowing me the time that I need. Thank you, Chamuel and Raphael."

Activate Your Angels.

Wash your sheets. You'll sleep better. You'll feel better. That's the literal side of this.

Figuratively 'washing your sheets' means getting all of the funky 'oils' and smells and gunk off. Get it all off and out of you. Then you'll be ready to start the new year fresh. Let's allow Raphael and Zadkiel to do our laundry.

"Raphael and Zadkiel, I'm doing my New Year prep, so in light and love please 'wash' out negativity and cover me in positivity. Thank you, Zadkiel and Raphael."

Activate Your Angels.

Post traumatic stress - Winter makes it worse. The fact that it's post holidays doesn't help either. I love Winter, but I know that I'm in the minority on that one except maybe for those who bask in the Summer climes.

Hyper sensitivity amps up for PTSD trauma survivors. Everything seems to set you on edge...and being cooped up is a recipe for explosions. Retrain your brain, diffuse yourself and your surroundings with the guidance of Jophiel and Michael.

"Jophiel and Michael, in light and love remove the fear and doubt that consumes me during this season. My mind gravitates towards those negative thoughts rather than logical, controlled processes. Thank you, Jophiel and Michel for illuminating ideas that try to undo me."

Activate Your Angels.

People say 'put yourself in the other person's shoes.' Nowadays we're too busy trying to stay in our own shoes that we don't give anyone else's a second thought.

Try it though.

Think of someone who is or isn't close to you. Then examine their life situation. What's going right? What's not going right? How are they dealing with life, in general?

Now examine that at a deeper level, looking at more of the intricacies of their life.

Zadkiel and Jeremiel assist you with this practice.

"Zadkiel and Jeremiel as I examine another person's life state, in light and love, point out the similarities and differences from mine. Then point me in the direction of moving towards the positives to improve my healing journey. Thank you, Zadkiel and Jeremiel."

Activate Your Angels.

'Marriage and/or relationships are a 50/50 proposition.' No, they're not. They can't be.

Each party involved carries a different energy than the other. There will be times when they match up, and there will be times when they don't.

Example: If one person gets sick or has a bad day or is overwhelmed - their energy drops. That means that the other person probably needs to step up to keep life afloat.

If both find themselves with diminished energy it gets trickier. There can be a way to work through this though.

Raphael and Samuel to the rescue here.

"Raphael and Samuel, both my partner and myself find ourselves in the negative energy bank and are in need of a boost. In light and love, enlighten one or both of us as to how we can fill in gaps, raising our positivity, vitality and motivation to where we can still function effectively. Thank you, Raphael and Samuel."

Activate Your Angels.

Human nature generally draws people to those who exude confidence. It appears as charisma. We believe it to be a strength.

Professionals will tell you that often times, more often than not, those people lack self-confidence and they mask it in ego. You probably have more confidence than they do.

They might excel at something, but inside they're a puddle of insecure mush.

Haniel, Chamuel and Zadkiel are out there revealing those inner selves.

"Haniel, Chamuel and Zadkiel, in light and love, disclose to me those who command a spotlight behind an inner being of self-doubt. I need this so that I find my own way and don't live vicariously through them or dream of a life like theirs which is built on falsehoods. Thank you, Haniel, Chamuel and Zadkiel.

Activate Your Angels.

Paul Simon said recently in an interview, "Acceptance of less is life." He was talking about losing his hearing and what that meant to him.

Very wise words.

Reality tells us that the minute we are born we start to die. As we move along that journey we find that the need for more, or even what we already have, diminishes. It's quite freeing.

Jophiel helps us with understanding life. Metatron enlightens us. Uriel opens us to new ideas. And Raphael helps us to find the silver linings.

"Jophiel, Metatron, Uriel, and Raphael, in light and love open me and enlighten me to the wonders of my life that live not of this world. Help me to find the gift in every situation that shows me that less of this world means more in the other world that's within us. Thank you, Jophiel, Metatron, Uriel, and Raphael."

Activate Your Angels.

'And' or 'But.' These two words can change your whole outlook on life.

'And' gives you direction. 'But' stops you in your tracks.

Example: I will start on my healing journey and I will make every effort. I will start on my healing journey but...

The 'but' slows you down, oftentimes stopping you all together. Do you feel it? It becomes an excuse not to do something.

Michael and Gabriel join together in helping you to choose wisely.

"Michael and Gabriel, in light and love, when I am faced with the choice between 'and' or 'but' in processing my healing, strengthen me and send me encouragement and motivation to take the positive path...to choose the 'and'. Thank you, Michael and Gabriel."

Activate Your Angels.

Common sense: 'Sound and prudent judgment based on a simple perception of the situation or facts.' So says Merriam Webster.

When you are lacking common sense, it can cause frustration and sometimes disappointment.

Let me ask you this: Did you ever think that your angels can help you with this?

I believe they can, and Haniel and Zadkiel thrive on helping.

"Haniel and Zadkiel, in light and love come into my heart and mind with your messages that help me to make better decisions...to see things more broadly rather than through tunnel vision. Thank you, Haniel and Zadkiel."

Activate Your Angels.

One of my top three favorite four-letter words is 'hope.'

It got even better when a friend of mine wore a t-shirt that said, "H.O.P.E. Hold On Pain Ends."

If I don't get any other message across through the angels I want that to be the one. It's so simple.

Yet there are times when having hope is so hard to do. Trauma survivors, strugglers, pretty much everyone loses hope at some point.

That's when I've always looked to my angels to help me. Michael's strength linked with Zachariel's strength shine bright.

"Michael and Zachariel, in light and love, shine your light-filled messages on me when I think the pain is too much. I need the strength of your messages to keep holding on until a brighter day. Thank you, Michael and Zachariel."

Activate Your Angels.

Expectations can defeat even the strongest let alone those of us who fight the battles of trauma.

Always anticipating the next event, the next moment, the next message, finds us losing sight of today.

We do need to be mindful of our celestial messages coming through. We need to do that in the moment, though.

Raphael's gift of finding the positive in every situation combined with Metatron's enlightening messages and Jophiel's unlimited capacity for understanding come in handy.

"Raphael, Metatron, and Jophiel—slowing down and savoring the moment are needed for my out-of-control expectations. As I progress in my healing journey, in light and love, flood me with messages that guide me in remaining in today and not worrying about tomorrow. Thank you, Raphael, Metatron, and Jophiel."

Activate Your Angels.

According to Aristotle, 'the virtuous person alone can attain happiness, and the virtuous person can never be miserable in the deepest sense, even in the face of misfortune which keeps him from being happy or blessed.'

What Aristotle means is that we hold an element within us that we have greater control over (virtue) compared to what we have lesser control over such as relationship, health, wealth, and so on.

Moral character containing courage, generosity, justice, friendship and citizenship compromise virtue.

As we all walk our healing journey, then we can turn to Michael and Uriel and Haniel.

"Michael, Uriel and Haniel, in light and love, bring forth these qualities in me that I might expand them into a more virtuous life and in so doing find greater happiness. Thank you, Michael, Uriel and Haniel."

Activate Your Angels.

I recently read an interesting article in Scientific American titled, "Do We Actually 'Hear' Silence?".

The finding—silence is the absence of sound. It feels like we can hear it. BUT if it really isn't a sound, yet we can hear it, then hearing is more than just sound.

I bring this up in relation to hearing angels. This study confirms that as humans we are able to relate to things not present to us.

Zadkiel and Laviah prompt us on these moments.

"Zadkiel and Laviah, in light and love guide me through this unseen journey of messages from you and all angels. Thank you, Zadkiel and Laviah."

Activate Your Angels.

Carl Jung said, "Thinking is difficult. That's why people judge."

Very wise words. We are so bombarded with information, especially when we're on our phones and other technology all the time. We don't have time to think for ourselves.

That's not good for us, and that's not good for the world.

We were uniquely created and in that we uniquely should be thinking individually. When we don't, we open ourselves up to trauma because our inner core, our soul, our being knows who we are. Given enough time we lose sight of who we really are.

We need Jophiel and Jeremiel and Uriel and Zadkiel to set us right.

"Jophiel, Jeremiel, Uriel and Zadkiel, I know that I am my own unique self...different from everyone else. In light and love, guide me back to who I am, who I was meant to be without interference from the world. That way I can carry out my purpose in this life and heal the trauma this has caused. Thank you, Jophiel, Jeremiel, Uriel and Zadkiel."

Activate Your Angels.

Hearing voices? You're not alone. It's believed that 3 - 10% of the population see visions and hear voices. That can increase to 75% if you include other similar experiences like someone calling your name.

I have had angels call my name. I have seen things that may or may not be of this world. I'm not crazy. I'm not schizophrenic.

Many of you feel alone in this. Some face prejudice. Still others feel like they're mentally ill.

While schizophrenia does afflict some, I believe that many of us are just sensitive to supernatural energies. I clearly communicate with angels, and my family and friends know that I'm as sane as can be.

So, first of all you need Michael. You also need to call in Uriel and Zadkiel to guide you in receiving these messages.

"Michael, Uriel and Zadkiel, in light and love, please help me to discern the origin of these voices and possibly even visions. Then guide me in their messages that the meaning or the mission can be carried out. Thank you, Michael, Uriel and Zadkiel.

Activate Your Angels.

[For those of you who are concerned please seek professional help.]

Swedish death cleaning. Sound ominous, doesn't it? It comes from the Swedish word *dostadning.*

It's a real thing, though. You're probably more familiar with it than you think.

Part of my family origins are Swedish. I get this. It's not scary.

It's actually a great way for trauma survivors and those who struggle to deal with their anxiety and even depression.

It's all about clearing and organizing your living space so that it's useful for anyone needing to let go of something, not just with someone's passing.

Laviah, Jermiel, and Chamuel create a great space for you to tackle this.

"Laviah, Jeremiel, and Chamuel, in my healing I know that I still need to declutter both physical and mental/emotional items that are holding me back. In light and love, help me to accept that I don' t need to keep things to preserve a memory nor should I in regards to my trauma. These things carry emotions and some bring no worth to me. Thank you, Laviah, Jeremiel, and Chamuel."

Activate Your Angels.

I grew up with a boy who was bullied because he always had a runny nose.

Back then no one realized that it was allergies. Now we know.

Because of his condition he was ridiculed, isolated and made to feel ashamed. It always broke my heart, because I would see the hurt and sadness in his eyes.

The last that I heard he went on to become a successful businessman whose philanthropy helped many people.

If you've ever been bullied you can turn it around for good.

I've called on Raphael, Metatron, and Chamuel when my bullying days reared their ugly heads.

"Raphael, Metatron and Chamuel, in light and love, provide me with the insight to see the gift in every situation. Allow me to take that positivity and build my self-esteem to heal me emotionally and help others. Thank you, Raphael, Metatron, and Chamuel."

Activate Your Angels.

Trauma grief. Not a common phrase, but a real one nonetheless.

When my first husband passed away I felt all of the old emotions and feelings flood back to me. The fear, the anger, the anxiety - everything that you feel when you're in a traumatic relationship.

I did therapy, but at the time of his passing grief still stepped in, and the old memories came flooding back. They also came back for my kids - now grown adults with their own families.

Traumatic relationships leave long-lasting scars. Doesn't mean that you can't work through them. Thanks to my earlier therapy I've been doing that.

Metatron, Chamuel, Samuel, and Jeremiel have been my guiding lights.

"Metatron, Chamuel, Samuel and Jeremiel, in light and love, show me how to work through my traumatic relationship history, whether in grief or just to move forward. I know that I can heal from this with your help. Thank you, Metatron, Chamuel, Samuel and Jeremiel.

Activate Your Angels.

Psychologists tell us that 'othering' is a kind of ignorance that's buried deep within our human motivations. It's the act of highlighting our differences, and then using those differences as justification for boundaries and hierarchies.

We do this because our human nature needs to make sense of the world. When we organize by 'us vs them' we're able to find our social identity. It allows us to take our world from complex to simple.

It also sets up division and struggles for everyone. It echoes of 'lumping and labeling'.

Instead, we should focus on our positive similarities and shared goals and visions for betterment. When we do that we come together to build our world rather than attack it.

Uriel, Zadkiel, Metatron, Zachariel, Jophiel, Laviah, Jeremiel, Raguel, and Haniel work together to overcome the dark and create this.

The Spartan life or code exists. It's not some ancient, archaic myth.

It centers around a life of discipline, obedience and courage.

From there, like many other things, it can go in many different directions. We're going to focus on this for our purposes with life struggles.

Life doesn't guarantee us freedom from conflict or struggle. We do have the power though to minimize it if we go about our lives in a disciplined and courageous way. The obedience comes in, remaining steadfast to the discipline you've set out for yourself and the courage that you've established.

Michael emanates courage and Chamuel emanates discipline to allow Jophiel's goal-setting to occur.

"Michael, Chamuel and Jophiel, I need you to join forces on this to get me prepped on my journey to minimize the things of this world that diminish the light and love that I am meant to project. Thank you, Michael, Chamuel, and Jophiel."

Activate Your Angels.

"Uriel, Zadkiel, Metatron, Zachariel, Jophiel, Laviah, Jeremiel, Raguel, and Haniel, in light and love, bombard me with your messages to help me engage in the necessary work to realize the shared healthy vision for my world. This is a gargantuan task that I know will aid me with my struggles as well as others. Thank you, Uriel, Zadkiel, Metatron, Zachariel, Jophiel, Laviah, Jeremiel, Raguel, and Haniel."

Activate Your Angels.

Does this sound like you?

No time for yourself, always feeling like you've got sandpaper rubbing you in the wrong direction, nothing seems to be going right, too much drama surrounding you....should I go on?

You need to take some alone time and focus on you - what's got you in a stranglehold; what's subliminally occupying your life; and why you can't break free.

Haniel and Sandalphon can help get you grounded and balanced once again.

"In light and love, Haniel and Sandalphon, please get me on your ongoing chat so that I might figure out my self-care for all stages of my life, as I progress through this life. Thank you, Haniel and Sandalphon."

Activate Your Angels.

Recently I was helping a family to clean out someone's home. The person had passed.

We found so many pennies and dimes all over the house to the point that we accumulated a bag full.

Finding pennies and dimes signifies that angels are present. Given the whole situation around the passing of this person's death it was comforting to receive those coins.

Oftentimes when we're out and about we'll randomly come across a penny or dime just laying on a sidewalk or on a floor in a store. That's a sign to you that your angel decided to make their presence known to you.

Look around you. Think about that moment in your life. Your angel wants to get a message through to you.

If you don't understand at that moment, just keep watching for signs. Angels can be persistent in getting their messages through to you.

Thank you, Angels.

Activate Your Angels.

People ask me "which do you prefer officiating - weddings or funerals?"

My response: "funerals."

Weddings bring out the egos of everyone. Funerals bring out the souls of everyone.

It's raw emotion. It's real. It's a time of self-revelation - taking stock of one's life.

It's a good thing.

Life assessment should be done more often than when grieving. It should be done anytime we have a 'life' change or in preparation of one.

Jophiel and Haniel make a great combo to assist you with this.

"Jophiel and Haniel, just like I evaluate my finances, my friends, my career, I want to assess my heart and my mind regularly. In light and love, guide me in achieving these life enlightenments. Thank you, Jophiel and Haniel."

Activate Your Angels.

Gaslighting trauma boils down to emotional abuse. It's a deliberate humiliation. A gaslighter's intent is to take control of how you feel about yourself and it's toxic.

Narcissists most commonly engage in gaslighting to manipulate, dominate, and control relationships. In order to free yourself from this abuse you must recognize it.

Zadkiel and Jophiel combine forces to guide and support you.

"Zadkiel and Jophiel, in light and love, I need you to help me set boundaries, find the words to speak to take back my control, and gather support from friends and family that I might break free from this abuse. Thank you, Zadkiel and Jophiel."

Activate Your Angels.

When the brain doesn't sleep, which is a common occurrence when you're anxious, depressed, hyper-aroused, etc., you experience cognitive loss.

The cognitive loss comes in the form of lost or false memories, hallucinations, cerebral shrinkage, and even brain damage. Trauma affects our brain function probably the most.

Our brains and our bodies require sleep for healthy function. When we don't receive enough sleep, growth gets stymied.

Zadkiel and Raphael bring you healthy suggestions to help you sleep.

"Zadkiel and Raphael, my sleep is often disrupted and at times non-existent. In light and love, help me find and use the right combination of physical and mental routines to take me into restful, healthy slumber. Thank you, Zadkiel and Raphael."

Activate Your Angels.

Emotional murder is a real thing and causes great psychological trauma. It's sometimes referred to as soul murder.

It's a systematic destruction of someone via psychological and emotional abuse. Often times, but not always, this could involve a married partner having an affair. Whatever the reason, it involves lying and deception, and requires professional help and removal from the situation.

Jophiel and Michael should be called upon.

"Jophiel and Michael, I need courage and clarity, strength and mental protection to bring myself back to life. In light and love help me restore my soul...my essence through professional resources. Thank you, Jophiel and Michael."

Activate Your Angels.

Most of us grew up being read nursery rhymes. Most of them just seemed to be entertaining with a simple lesson to be learned. In reality most of those nursery rhymes hold secret meaning.

What started out as dissident folk songs about current events of the time or the abhorrent conduct of figureheads, actually hold messages within the lines. They tell of everything from cruelty and execution to greed and immorality...and more.

So, why am I telling you this?

Because oftentimes the appearance of innocence masquerades as a smoke screen for more sinister happenings. It's a warning to us, especially as trauma survivors or those who struggle with life. We need to be true to ourselves and trust our guts for appropriate healing.

Samuel and Zachariel guide us through the maze.

"Samuel and Zachariel, healing from trauma can be a struggle unto itself. In light and love, I need your direction to steer me clear of destructive and harmful healing means, and point me in the direction of harmonious methods. Thank you, Samuel and Zachariel."

Activate Your Angels.

Sheep follow. They are not leaders.

There's a new buzzword now - Electric Sheep.

Depending on who you're talking to it means several different things, but they all lead back to AI - Artificial Intelligence.

AI possesses a quagmire. It's very easy to be sucked into its charm, its information, and its misinformation. It's like the sheep blindly following the wolf in sheep's clothing.

Gabriel and Uriel can help you discern the pitfalls.

"Gabriel and Uriel, I find myself attracted to the AI world to the point where I might be losing my way. In light and love, direct me to a safe path as I explore this phenomenon so that I don't lose myself along the way. Thank you, Gabriel and Uriel."

Active Your Angels.

One of my biggest pet peeves involves people who constantly interrupt others and won't let them speak. For me it's maddening. Is it for you?

Because of this, professionals have started offering several communication tools to counter this social malady.

They include such things as asking to offer a different perspective or apologizing for interrupting. (That's interesting.)

They offer 'excusing' yourself as you interject and pointing out that you have something worthy of the conversation.

Using 'joiners' like "while we're on that topic" or asking to share an idea or clarifying the other person's point gets your voice into the mix.

Gabriel and Zachariel would love to join your conversations.

"Gabriel and Zachariel, in light and love, with internal strength prompt me when to speak up and help me form the appropriate interjection to allow my voice to be heard. Thank you, Gabriel and Zachariel."

Active Your Angels.

What drives curiosity?

Some would say that it comes from experiences that create a sensation of uncertainty or perceived unpleasantness. Huh?

According to professionals, that can include environment, fear, technology and/or assumptions. But those things lead to a decrease in curiosity.

We need curiosity, though, if we want to learn new things, have relationships, and gain knowledge. In other word those four factors isolate us.

We need Samuel, Gabriel, Metatron, Chamuel and Jeremiel to cut through this.

"Samuel, Gabriel, Metatron, Chamuel and Jeremiel, in light and love, show me how to lower these factors in my life, fear, technology, assumptions and anything environmental, that stagnate my curiosity for life and for the world. I don't want to be alone and miss what life offers me. Thank you, Angels."

Activate Your Angels.

We've all been given a purpose in life. Sometimes the vision or direction of the purpose gets blurred.

You can regain that focus and boost your positivity and motivation by doing a few simple things.

Michael and Uriel guide you on this jumpstarting journey.

"Michael and Uriel, in light and love, clarify and motivate me to seek out time for mental health respite to allow for inspiration and work on goals in small batches. And keep me connected to others who value my contributions in life. Thank you, Michael and Uriel."

Activate Your Angels.

SECTION FIVE

Images

Sit quietly with the image you've chosen, allowing it to speak to you without forcing any interpretations.

These images are about self-reflection and introspection. They prompt you to check in with your own feelings and thoughts. They focus on mental, emotional, and possibly physical well-being, as well as relationships and career/job aspects.

To apply these instructions to your life, take a moment to pause and consider how you're feeling mentally, emotionally, and physically. Reflect on your relationships and your current situation in terms of career or job. See if there are any areas where you feel you need to address or improve.

This practice can help you gain insight into your overall well-being and make any necessary adjustments to enhance your quality of life. If you don't receive any insights, try again later; perhaps it's not the right moment.

Remember, the angels may communicate differently each time you visit the image, but the message could also remain consistent.

Trust in the guidance of your angels and remain open to whatever messages they have to offer.

CH JODI M DEHN

CH JODI M DEHN

CH JODI M DEHN

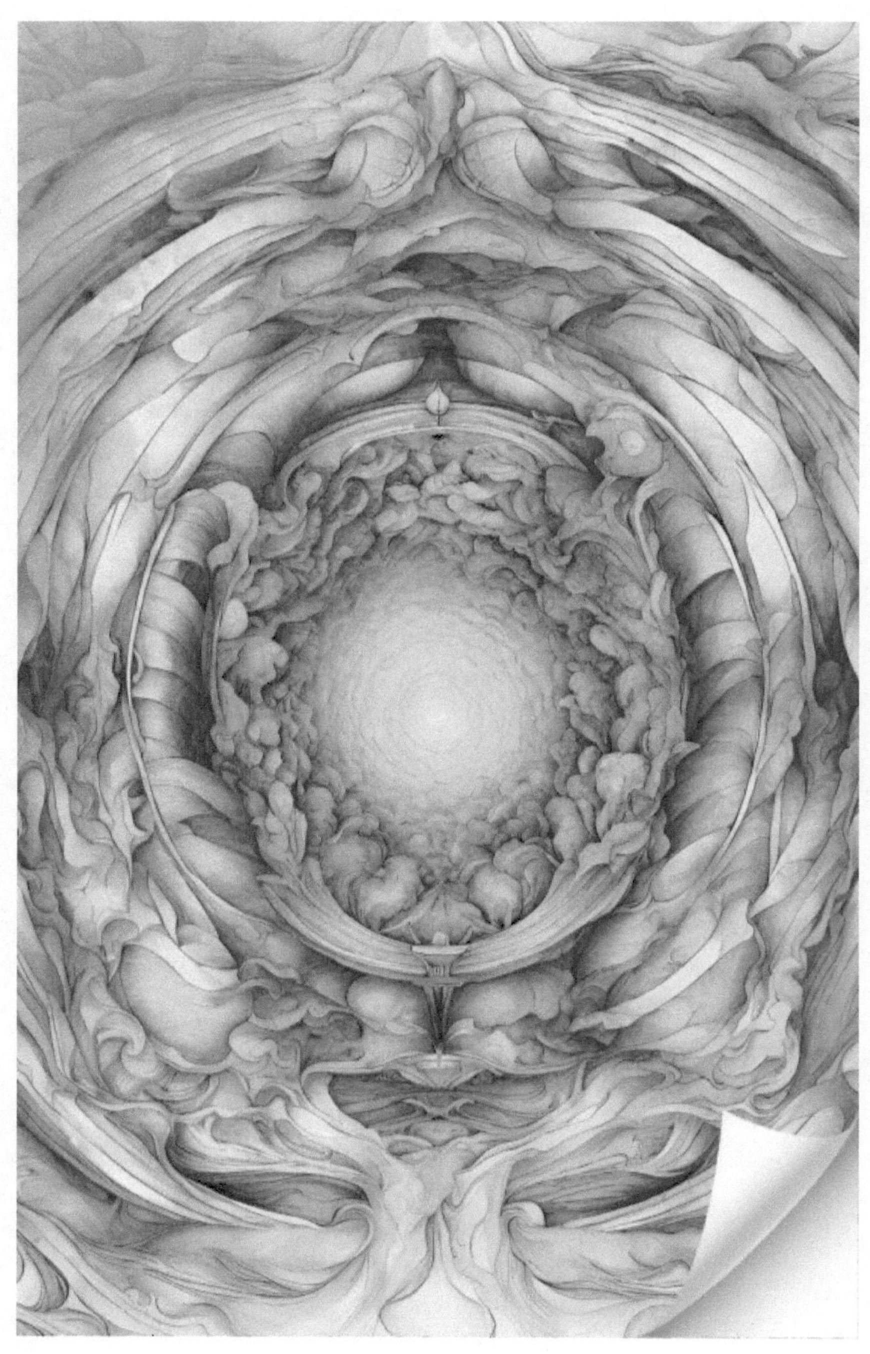

CH JODI M DEHN

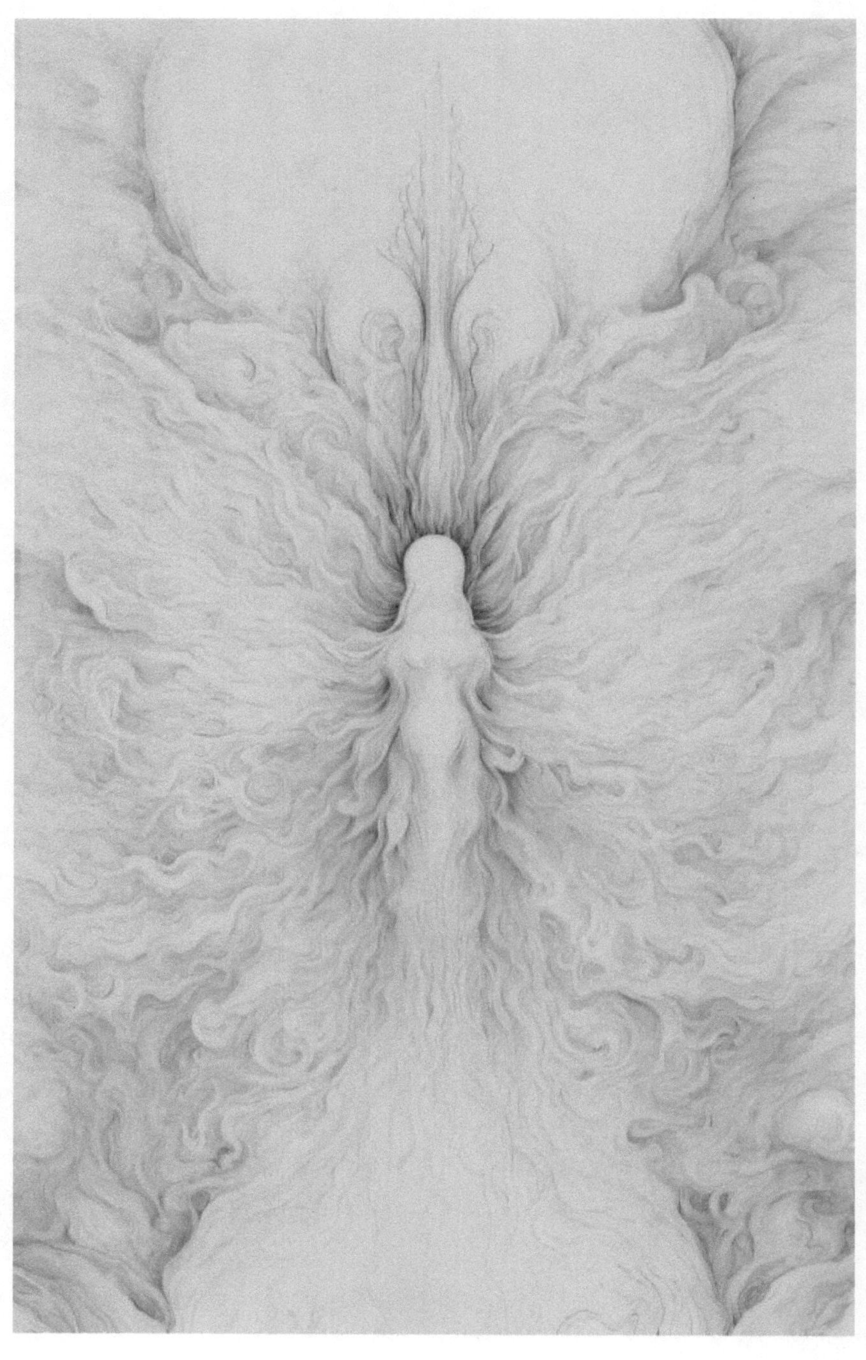

CH JODI M DEHN

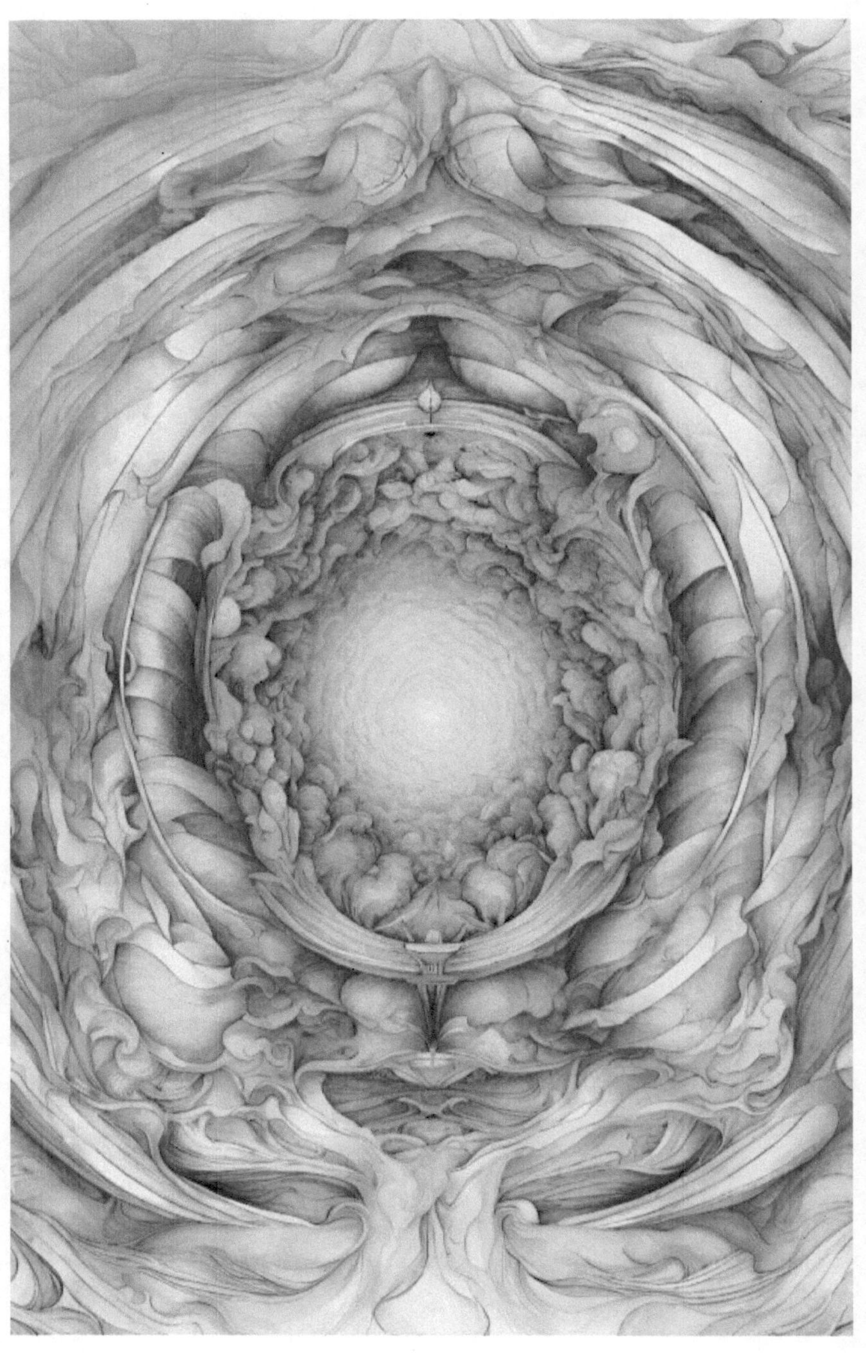

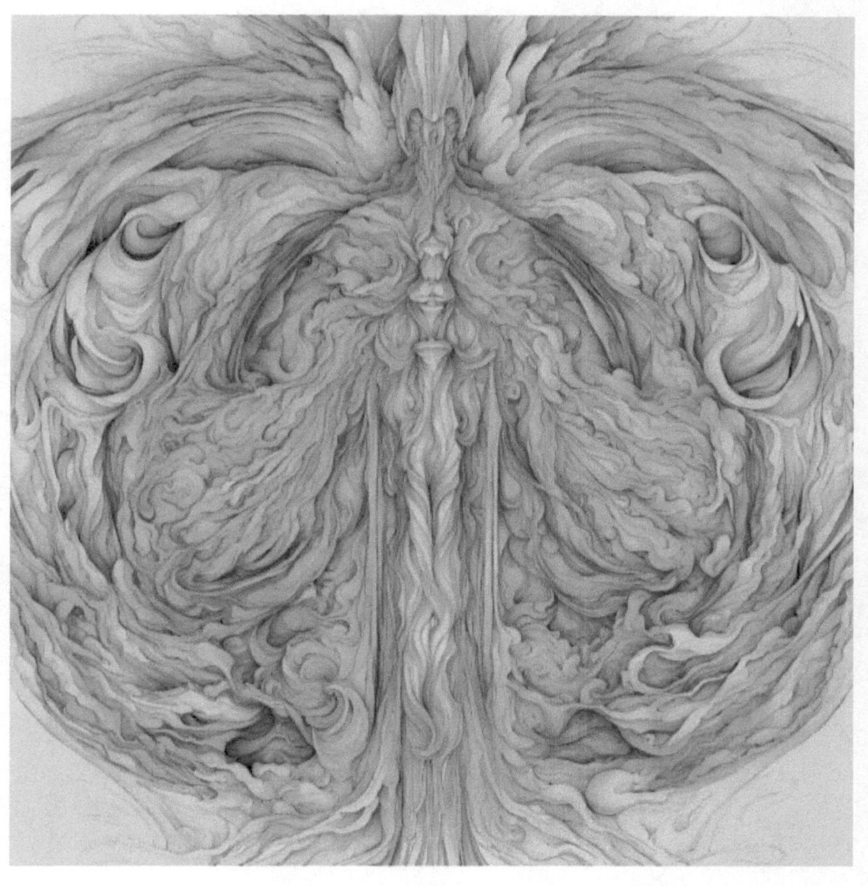

CH JODI M DEHN

CEREBRATE! ORACLE GUIDANCE FROM YOUR ANGELS

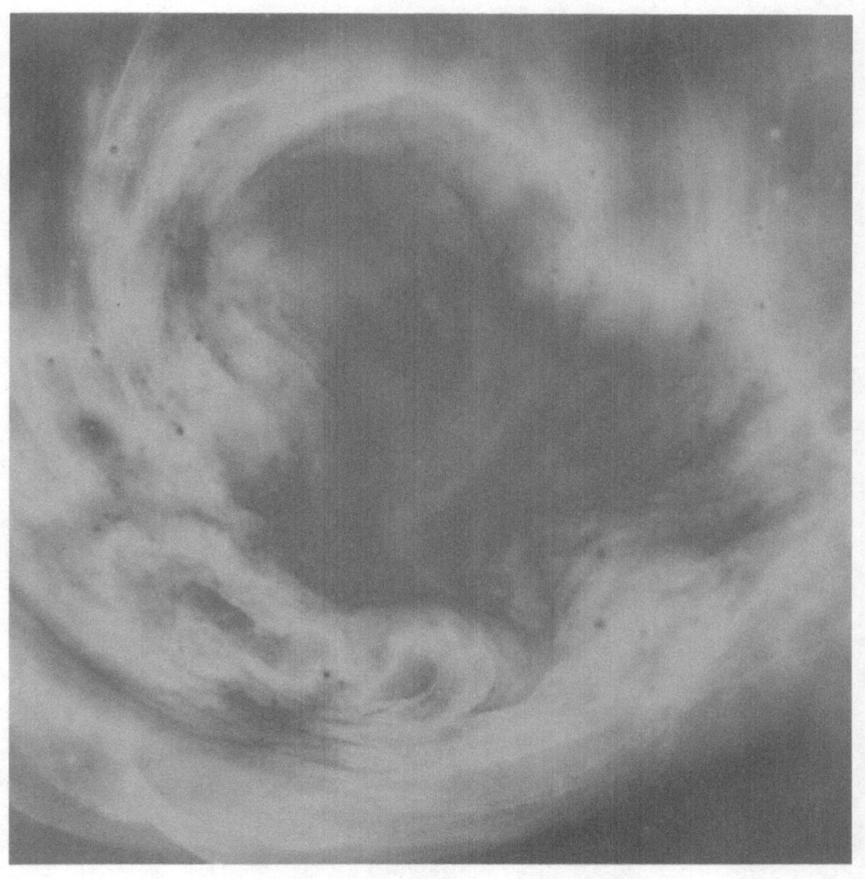

CH JODI M DEHN

CH JODI M DEHN

CH JODI M DEHN

CH JODI M DEHN

CH JODI M DEHN

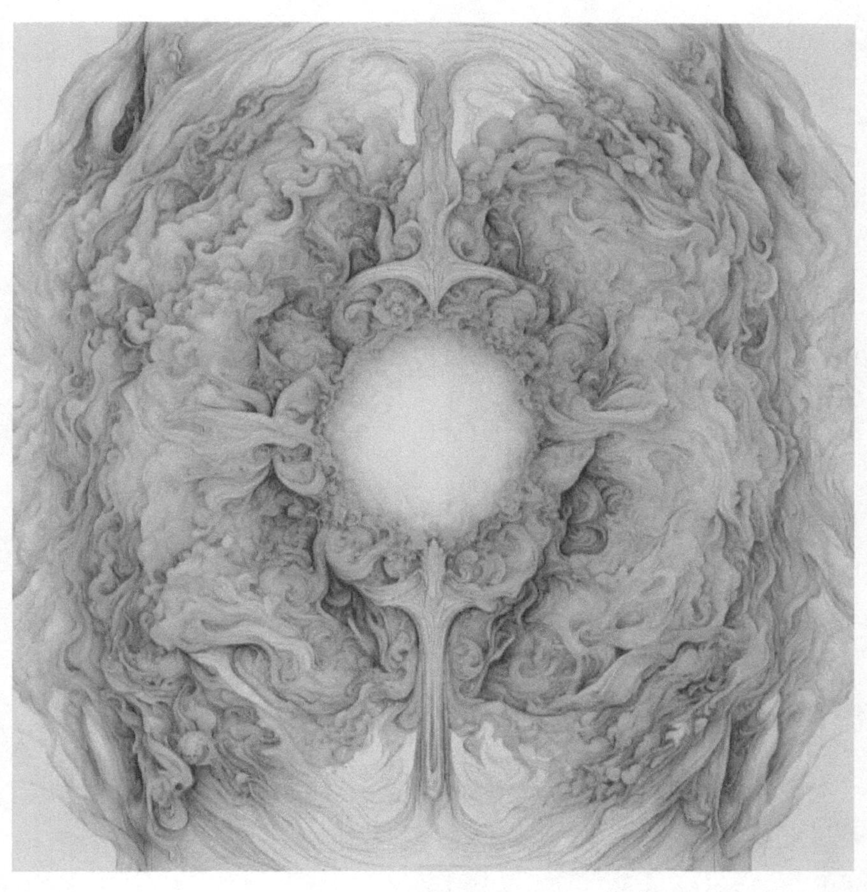

CH JODI M DEHN

CH JODI M DEHN

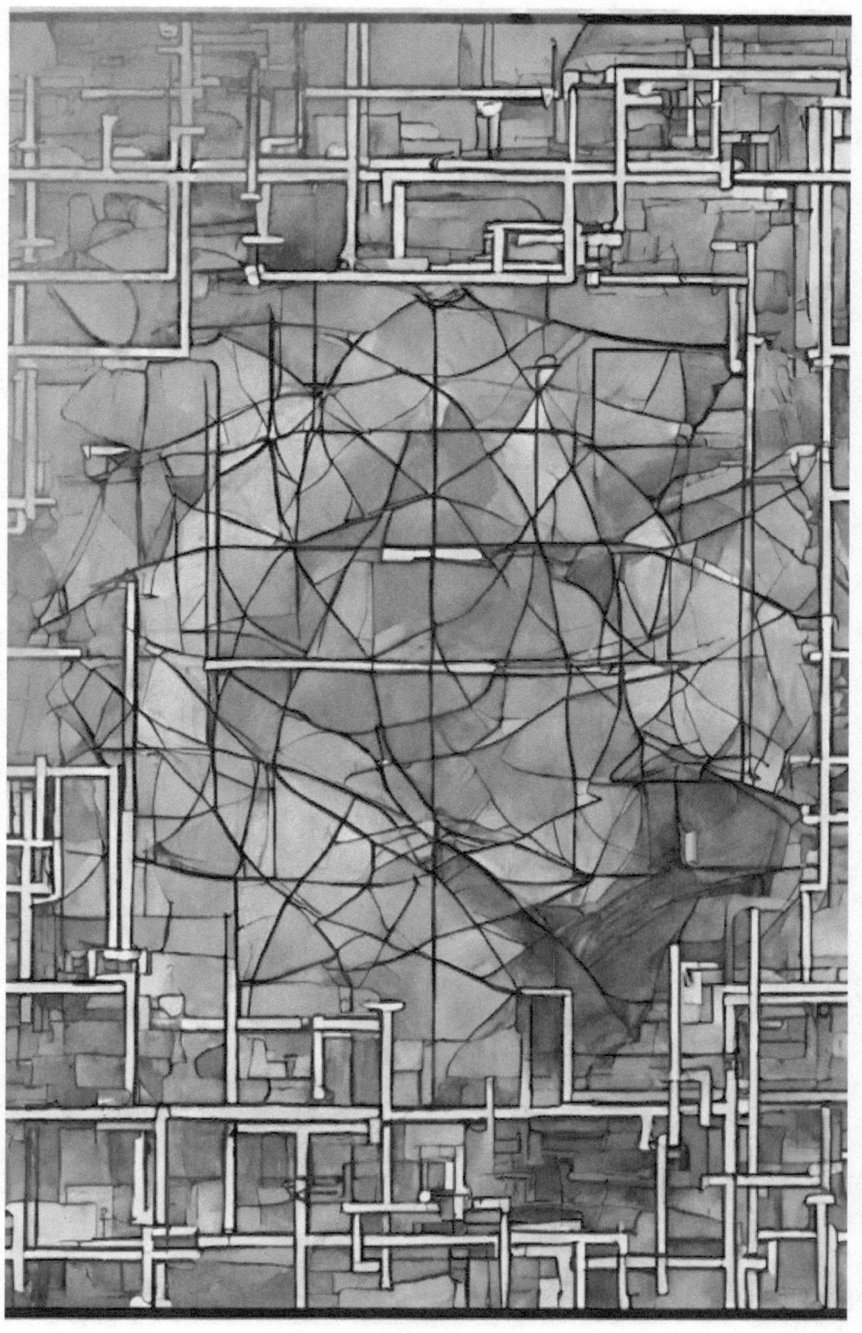

CH JODI M DEHN

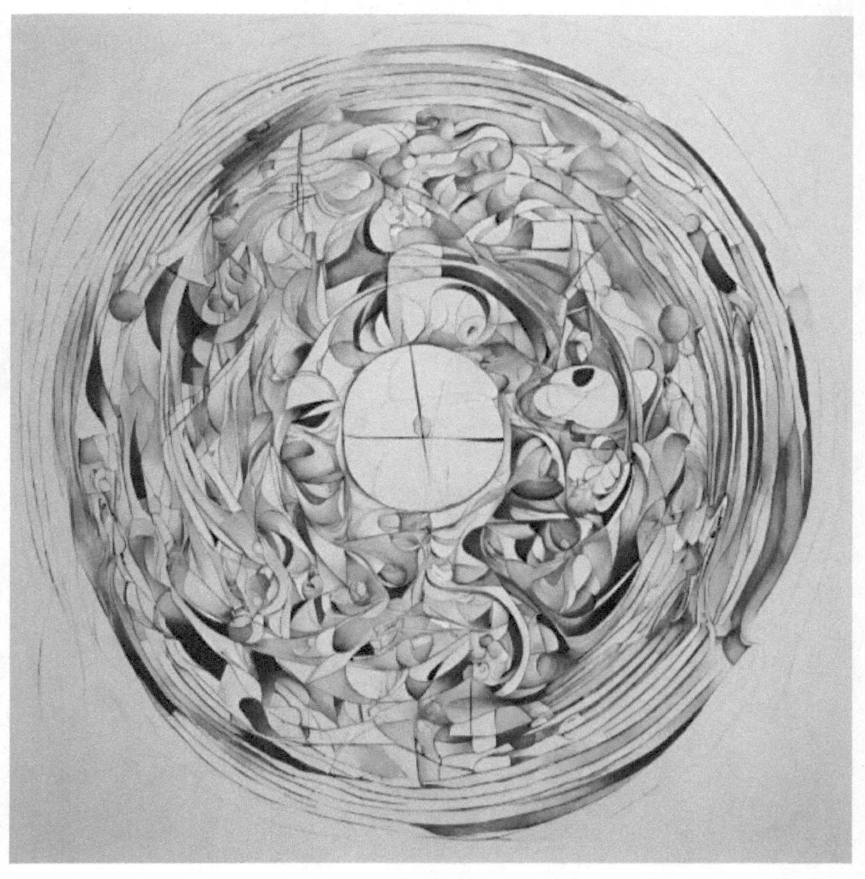

CH JODI M DEHN

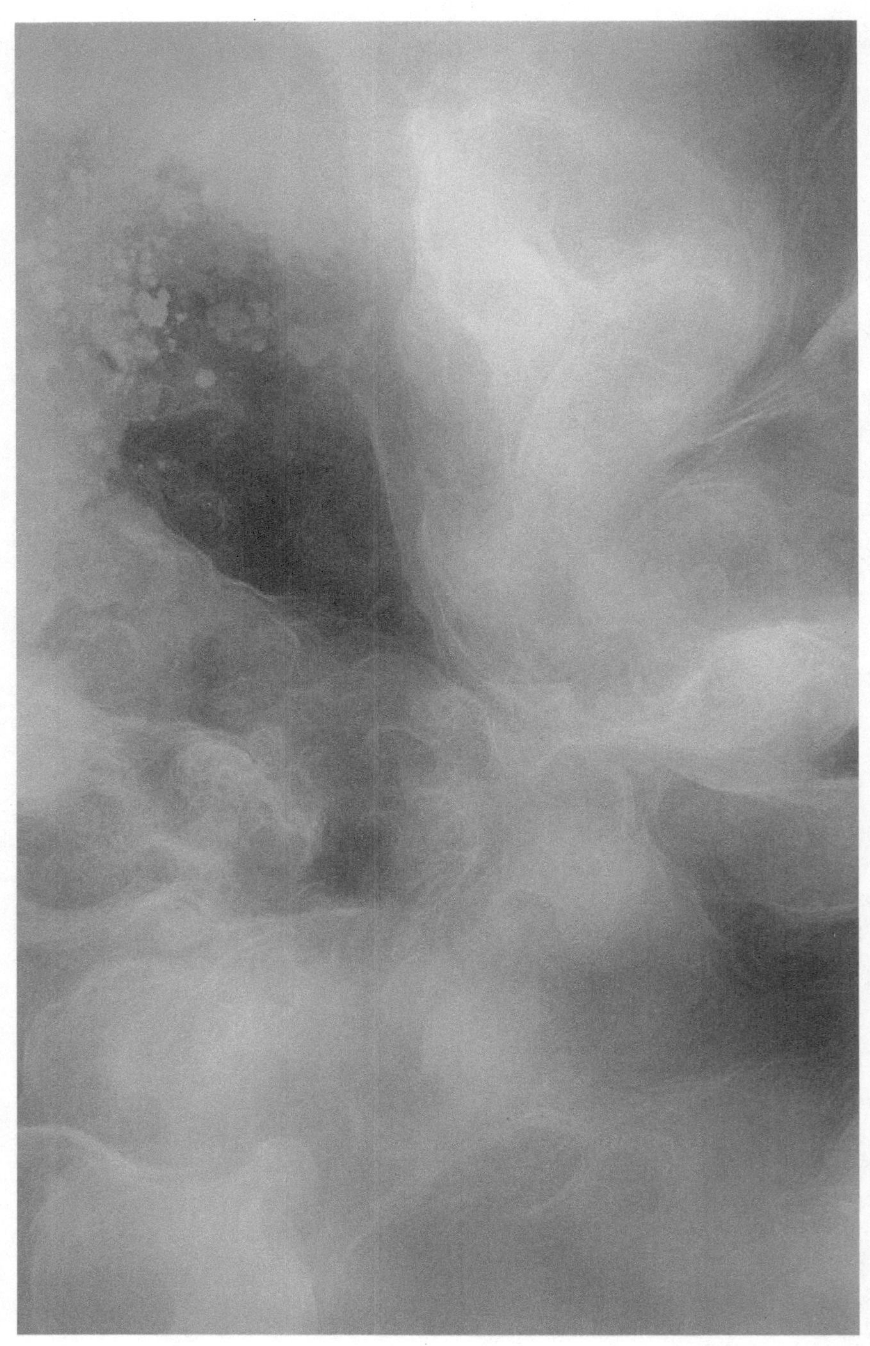

CH JODI M DEHN

CH JODI M DEHN

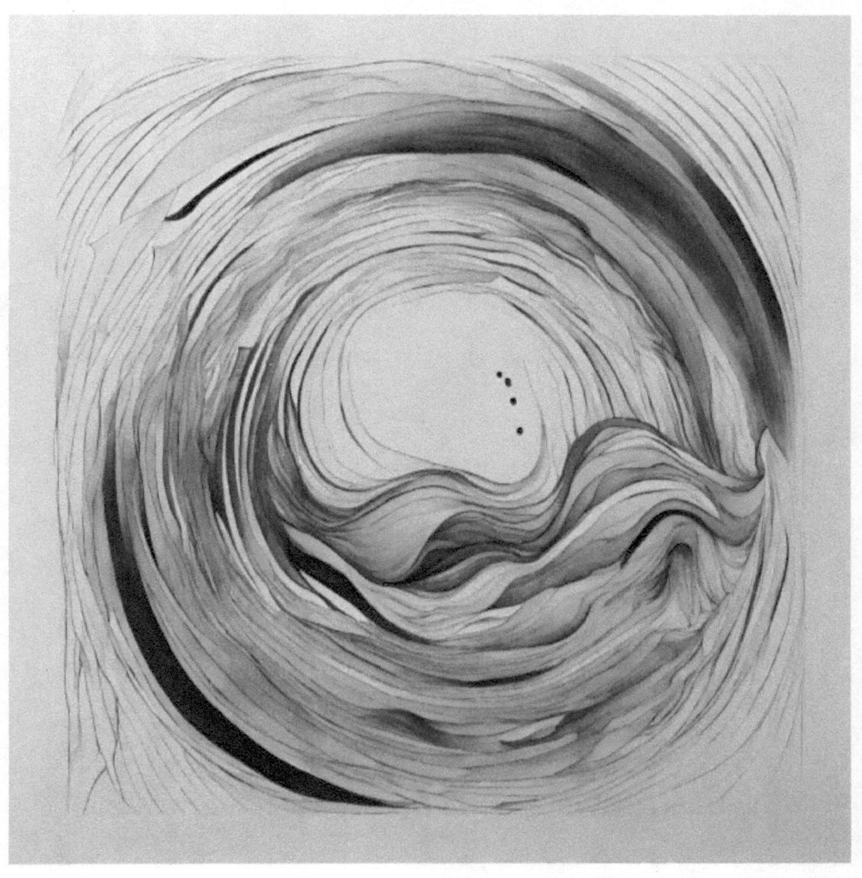

CH JODI M DEHN

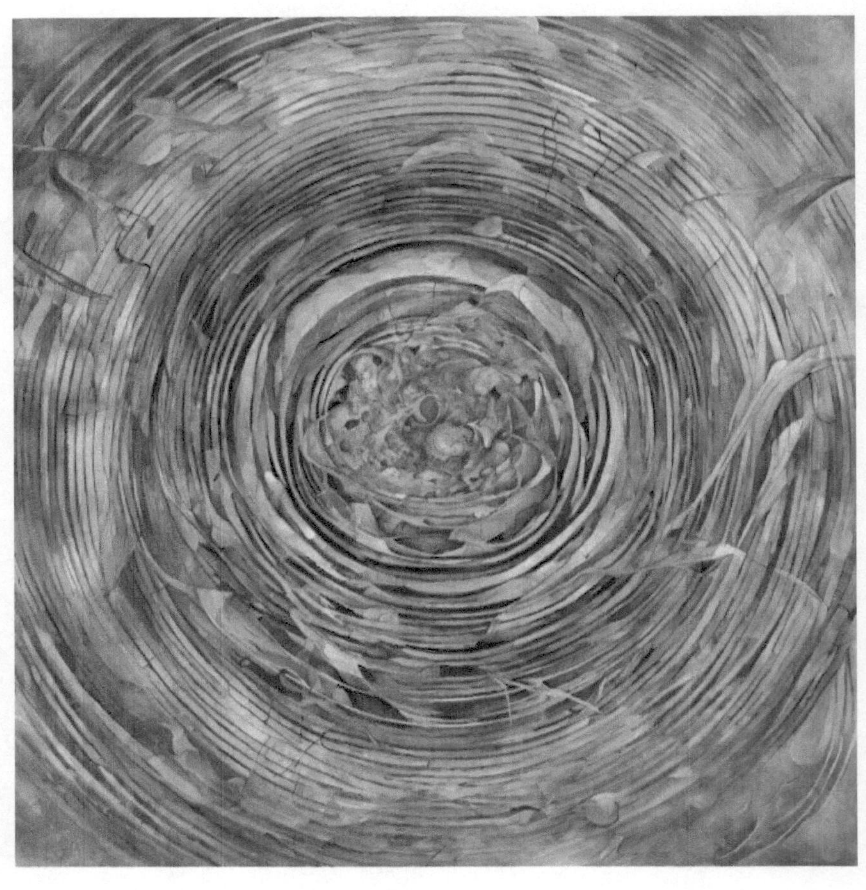

CH JODI M DEHN

CH JODI M DEHN

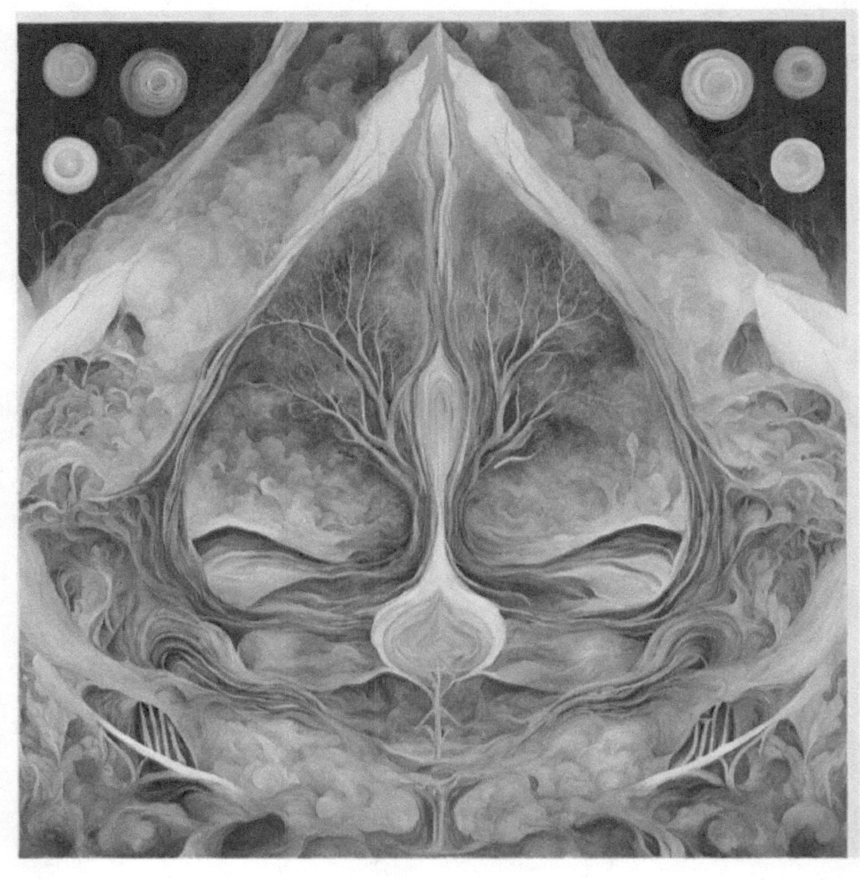

CH JODI M DEHN

CH JODI M DEHN

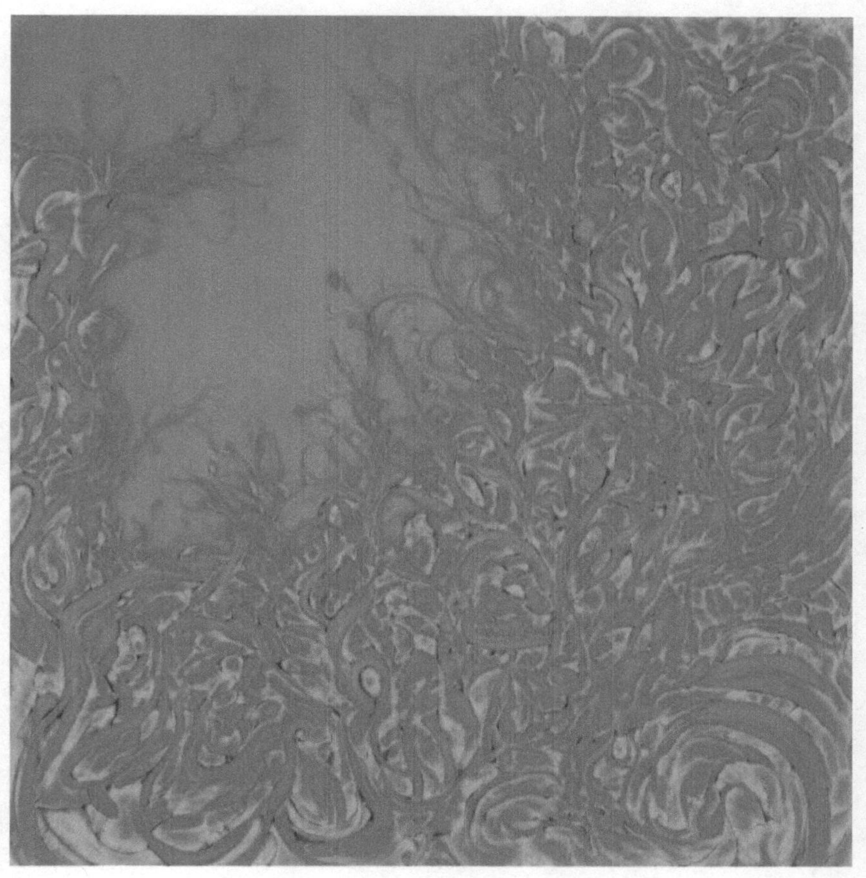

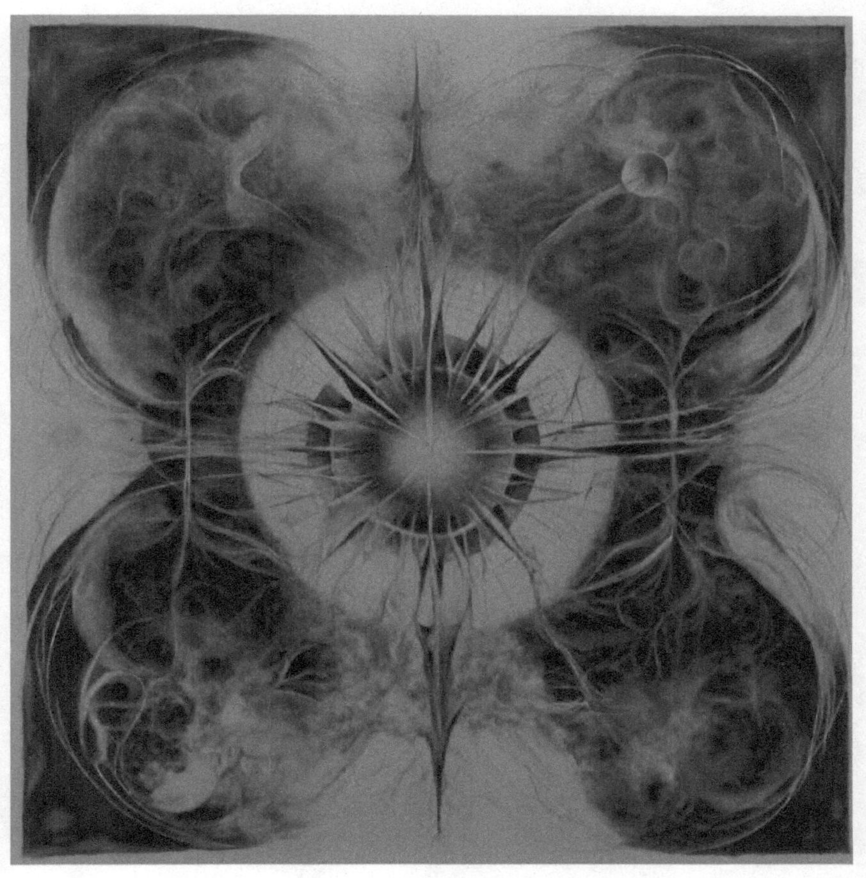

www.ingramcontent.com/pod-product-compliance
Lightning Source LLC
LaVergne TN
LVHW090609110826
845146LV00001B/322

* 9 7 9 8 9 8 9 8 5 2 4 1 3 *